WHITE FRAGILITY

WHY UNDERSTANDING RACISM CAN BE SO HARD FOR WHITE PEOPLE

Adapted for Young Adults

WHITE FRAGILITY

WHY UNDERSTANDING RACISM CAN BE SO HARD FOR WHITE PEOPLE

Adapted for Young Adults

ROBIN DIANGELO

ADAPTED BY TONI GRAVES WILLIAMSON AND ALI MICHAEL

BEACON PRESS · BOSTON

BEACON PRESS
Boston, Massachusetts
www.beacon.org

Beacon Press books
are published under the auspices of
the Unitarian Universalist Association of Congregations.

25 24 23 22   8 7 6 5 4 3 2 1

This book is printed on acid-free paper that meets the uncoated paper
ANSI/NISO specifications for permanence as revised in 1992.

Library of Congress Cataloging-in-Publication Data

Names: DiAngelo, Robin J., author. | Williamson, Toni Graves,
    editor, author. | Michael, Ali, editor, author.
Title: White fragility : why understanding racism can be so hard
    for white people : adapted for young adults / Robin DiAngelo ;
    adapted by Toni Graves Williamson and Ali Michael.
Description: Boston : Beacon Press, [2022] | Includes bibliographical
    references and index. | Summary: "A reimagining of the best-selling
    book that gives young adults the tools to ask questions, engage in
    dialogue, challenge their ways of thinking, and take action to create
    a more racially just world"—Provided by publisher.
Identifiers: LCCN 2022010696 | ISBN 9780807016091
    (hardback ; alk. paper) | ISBN 9780807016107 (ebook)
Subjects: LCSH: Racism—Juvenile literature. | Whites—Juvenile literature. |
    Race relations—Juvenile literature.
Classification: LCC HT1521 .D4862 2022 | DDC 305.8—dc23/eng/20220304
LC record available at https://lccn.loc.gov/2022010696

*To young people of all racial
backgrounds . . .
because we know that you will
change the world.*

CONTENTS

Reading this book is meant to be an opportunity to put on a new pair of lenses for looking at the world around you. It's not the kind of book to read through without stopping.

We encourage you to slow down, get a blank notebook for journaling, and take time to reflect as you read each chapter. Write down any thoughts and questions you have as you go. When you're finished, go back through your notebook and see whether you have new answers to your old questions. Or new questions about old ideas. There are "afterthoughts" at the end of each chapter, which can prompt journal reflections or discussions with friends.

As you move through this book there will be times that you may feel uncomfortable. You may have already felt that way before this page. Don't worry! Discomfort is a normal part of talking about race, particularly because so many people were taught not to do it. When you do talk about race and you feel discomfort, it's not a sign that something is wrong—it's actually a sign that you are doing something right.

Think about all the times that you have been in your discomfort zone—learning something new, going to a new place, meeting new people. Many experts believe that you can't learn without being uncomfortable. And yet, it's also true that our bodies often try to keep us comfortable. If we begin to feel discomfort, we might go into "fight, flight, or freeze" mode, which leads us to step back into our comfort zones. We might put down the book or the conversation that is pushing us into that discomfort zone, argue with the friend who is challenging us to think differently, and close the door on the discomfort. In this book, challenge yourself to **lean into that discomfort.**[1] It's precisely because race conversations are rare in our society that they are going to be uncomfortable. And that also makes them special. There is incredible potential for growth and change for those of us who are willing to stand together in our discomfort zones.

Journaling and engaging with the discussion questions will help you notice how your feelings and reactions change as you read. To help you track your body's reaction to this conversation, we offer a few guiding questions to return to when you feel the discomfort. When you become uncomfortable or perhaps disagree with what is being said consider the following questions:

Content Warning

When we were writing this book, we received feedback from well-intentioned readers who suggested that we may want to include content warnings in certain sections, particularly one where we mention sexual assault. We sat with this feedback and appreciated it, but we also questioned it. The truth is, there's a lot of material in this book that might make you uncomfortable, that *should* make *all of us* uncomfortable. First, as we have acknowledged, some people will be uncomfortable simply because it can be hard to talk about race. That's real. Second, we do mention sexual assault and rape, both in the modern context and in the context of enslavement. Both deserve a content warning. But third, we write in this book about how racism impacts People of Color. We write about innocent Black teenagers who have been killed or incarcerated. We write about the increased violence against Asian Americans during COVID-19. We write about the ways that Latinx people are made to be second-class citizens. We write about how Native people have been dispossessed of land, livelihood, and culture. The things we write about are traumatic. Racism is brutal.

So we want to issue a blanket content warning . . . for all of it. We have written this book in a way that we hope will introduce painful material slowly and intentionally. We want to support our readers in taking in the information without being overwhelmed. But we cannot pick and choose where to put content warnings because racism is traumatic. We hope reading this book will help you develop the skill and agility to challenge racism in ways that change this reality.

Other Things to Know About the Book

You'll notice that "we"—the narrator—is plural! *We* includes both Toni and Ali. We are a multiracial team (Toni is Black, Ali is White). Otherwise, this book is our collective adaptation of Robin DiAngelo's book *White Fragility*. It is an adaptation of her words and work, but it is not the same book. Here are some of the ways it is different:

- It has been adapted for young adults to include developmentally appropriate material in terms of language, examples, and concepts.
- The author and artist team is made up of one Black woman, one Black man, and two White women, who worked in consultation with Robin, a White woman.
- We have worked with youth readers, youth focus groups, and teachers to determine what material and language will be most relevant for a Young Adult adaptation.
- We have added images and drawings to help the concepts come alive on the page.
- This version includes a chapter on navigating media . . . social and otherwise.
- This version also includes a chapter on taking action. Once you understand white fragility, what can you do? You will find some answers in Chapter 10.
- As you flip through the book, you will see portraits of some of the scholars and activists whose work influenced Robin's theory of white fragility. Robin connects to other authors, citing them and honoring their work. And, like most authors, she helps readers see their work in a new light by putting a unique frame around the

whole. In this case, she uses her own experience and research to develop the concept of white fragility. We chose to highlight some of the scholars whose work Robin deeply respects, to give you a sense of the intellectual roots of this concept that you are learning.

- Throughout the book, Toni and Ali share personal stories. They are marked as such with the name of the author following the story. You will also see scripted quotes from Robin. These quotes are impactful statements that appear here exactly as they appeared in the original *White Fragility*.

Finally, you may notice that we don't start talking about white fragility in earnest until Chapter 4. That is because it's hard to understand white fragility without understanding where it comes from, what's underneath it, and why it's so powerful. The first half of the book will lay the foundation. Hang in there; your patience will be rewarded, we promise. The second half will help you identify white fragility, recognize the feelings underneath it, see how it impacts your capacity to contribute to racial justice, and decide what to do about it.

INTRODUCTIONS

Introduction from Robin DiAngelo, Author of *White Fragility*

I grew up in poverty, in a family in which no one was expected to go to college. I understood at an early age that the world was not a fair place, but I had only ever thought about how it was unfair to me. Like most White people, I lived a segregated life. My neighborhoods, my schools, my friends, and my teachers were all mostly White. At the same time, I believed I was completely open-minded when it came to race and that I knew all I needed to. Many White people thought this way, even though we didn't talk openly about race or study it in school beyond being told that Dr. Martin Luther King, Jr. had ended it. But one day I took a job that required me to lead discussions on racism in the workplace. This was the first time in my life that I had ever talked directly about race, and I had *never* discussed race before in a racially mixed group. My worldview was shaken to the core during these discussions as People of Color shared their experiences and challenged my limited understanding. I felt like a fish being taken out of water.

The contrast between the way People of Color experienced the world and the way I did showed me that I did not share the same reality with everyone around me. I realized that regardless of how I had always seen myself, I was deeply uninformed—even ignorant—when it came to the complexities of racism. This ignorance was not harmless; it impacted how I saw myself and how I related to others. It made me defensive when anyone challenged my self-image as a completely open-minded person with no bias whatsoever. I saw this same defensiveness in many other White people whenever our ideas about racism and our relationship to it were questioned. I began to call these reactions white fragility: the inability or refusal to tolerate the discomfort that comes from being racially challenged.

In 2011 I wrote an article explaining white fragility. The article went viral, and I began to get emails from around the world from people who told me I had put into words something they had seen or felt, and how that was so helpful. In 2018 I turned the article into a book that, again, resonated worldwide. What you are reading now is the next step—making that original book accessible to a younger range of readers.

Today it is hard to avoid talking about racism, and we are being required to have some basic knowledge about this urgent issue. I have been studying racism for over twenty years and have led conversations on race with thousands of people worldwide, including teachers and students. I have never met someone who didn't have an opinion on racism, and most of those opinions are very strong and emotional. I am quite sure that you—dear reader—have an opinion on racism. But having an opinion is not the same thing as being *informed*. Given how complex and sensitive the topic is, how long racism has been going on, and how much controversy surrounds it, this book asks you to "try on" the ideas it presents and be willing to slow down and make sure you understand an idea before you reject it. I can promise you that the journey will be fascinating and rich with insight!

Toni's Intro

As an educator for over twenty years, I have loved working with all ages and all races of students. When I run into an old student, I love seeing what they are up to now. Recently, I ran into Rebecca. She was a student that graduated a few years ago from the school where I work and has since graduated from college. My favorite question to ask former students is "So, how are you dismantling systems of oppression?" (You'll learn more about this idea later in the book.) Ultimately, I want to know what contributions they are making to fight racism. Unbeknownst to me, Rebecca was there to take my school's faculty on a tour of Philadelphia. But not just any tour. She and a friend from college had decided to create a company called Beyond the Bell. They lead tours of the city that tell the stories and contributions of People of Color, women, and queer folks who have been left out of many history books. Her answer to me that day was "I started this company!" Awesome.

As we have adapted this book, I have been thinking about all the young readers out there beyond the schools where I have worked who will gain access to some of the same tools Rebecca got that led her down that path. I thought of the many different ways that folks reading this book may be able to answer the question, "What contributions are you making to end racism?" I said yes to this project to increase the possibility of creating more anti-racist voices in our world from people taking action.

To prepare, I reread *White Fragility* and thought about how we were going to adapt it for Young Adult readers. I reflected on and reworked my own thoughts about social forces, the pillars of Whiteness, and White racial frames. I went to bed the night of May 24, 2020, excited about the possibility of finding ways to help younger people understand the important concepts presented in the book. So even though we were in the middle of a pandemic and I had spent the ten weeks before then social distancing, I felt a glimmer of hope and a fire that I had seen very little of in the weeks since the pandemic had started.

And then George Floyd was murdered the next day.

I asked myself, Why am I working so hard? Is anyone listening? Am I wasting my breath, my time, my energy?

Then came the protests. Folks were taking to the streets. People of all races. I started hearing from former classmates and coworkers who were checking in on me and asking me for resources. I saw former students on the frontlines in social media. That was when I realized the necessity of this book. Young people need a resource that speaks to them, and here was the opportunity. We hope the pages of this book give our readers chances to ask questions, engage in dialogue, and challenge their ways of thinking as we all navigate strategies to dismantle systems of inequity and racism. We hope that People of Color who choose to read this book feel validated and supported.

Recently, I got a message from a White person that I knew in high school. He wanted me to know that I had called him out on something he said that was racist when we were sixteen years old! I don't remember the incident, but he said that what he learned that day was the beginning of his journey in trying to do better. This was confirmation for me that having an opportunity to write the adaptation of this book was a window into more folks' lives. In the words of Maya Angelou, "When you know better, you do better!" We hope that this book helps folks adhere to those important words.

Ali's Intro

One thing I deeply appreciate about young adults today is that you care deeply about fairness, justice, and the world you are going to inherit. You have lived through a global pandemic, and you have seen what can happen when people and nations don't figure out how to work together. It seems almost second nature for you to challenge the binary gender boxes we've been given. You are growing up with an awareness of climate change that no generation before you had at your age. Your particular knowledge and experience of the world is unique and powerful. It is my hope that this book will support your journey toward developing the knowledge and skill to create a better, more racially just world.

If you are reading this book, then you are already ahead of where I was when I was your age. I grew up in the predominantly White suburbs of Pittsburgh and attended a high school that was 99 percent White. All my teachers, pre-K through twelfth grade, were White. My community and family thought that we were supposed to be colorblind and not talk about race—I believe that we felt this was how to be "good" White people.

It wasn't until college, when I was required to take a course on African American literature, that I started to realize how much my training to be colorblind was a block to learning about race. I found myself engaged in the material, but stumbling over saying aloud the simplest words like "White" or "Black" or "Afro Latina" or "Chinese American." I never knew what terms to use exactly, or in what order. Was I being offensive? Was I using an in-group term that was off limits to me as a White person? Because I had spent most of my life trying to be colorblind, everything was new to me: using racial language, looking at history and literature through a racialized lens, seeing the stark realities of racism. The worldview I had grown up with—in which I was taught to value small government and to believe that if you worked hard, you got ahead—was being pulled out from under me as I realized there were alternative explanations for everything I thought I knew.

Reading this book offers an opportunity to understand better why it can be so hard for White people to acknowledge racism, to talk about it, to hear about it, and to take action. We hope that for White people who are reading this, it presents a chance to look at yourself and your world a little differently, and to feel more empowered to take action as a result. We hope that for People of Color who are reading this, it will help you to name dynamics that you have experienced in your relationships with White people in ways that bring clarity and strategy to your own journey. To all readers, we hope that reading this book will help balance the burden of acting against racism; that People of Color will feel less weight on their shoulders because their White peers know better how to share the load.

It's an honor to be on this journey with you!

Chapter 1

WHY TALKING ABOUT RACE CAN BE SO HARD FOR WHITE PEOPLE

In my house, we talked about Black people in the light of day. We cheered for the Black family on Family Feud. We learned all the heroes of Black history. But if we wanted to talk about White people, we whispered: "White people." —Toni

The first time I heard this story from Toni, I laughed so hard because we didn't talk about race in my house. And we didn't talk about being White. But if the topic of Black people ever came up, we knew enough not to say it aloud. We whispered: "Black people." —Ali

Let's be clear, talking about race can be hard for everyone. It's awkward, you don't want to say the wrong thing, your words might be misconstrued, you might make someone uncomfortable, you may be seen as too angry or too ignorant. Especially in multiracial spaces, talking about race can feel like a land mine. But talking about race can be *uniquely* hard for White people. There are multiple reasons why it can be hard, but this chapter will cover two:

First, White people are taught to see themselves as raceless, which means they are taught that race and racism have nothing to do with them.

Second, White people are put at the top of the racial hierarchy in the US, which makes it hard to see that very hierarchy.

These two reasons are interrelated. If you don't know you have a race, or you think racism has nothing to do with you, then you are unlikely to even see the racial hierarchy, much less think you should be involved in challenging it.

This chapter will explore these two main points. By the end of the chapter, readers should have a clear picture of why talking about race can be so hard for White people and why racism won't change until White people learn to do it anyway.

White People Are Taught to See Themselves as Raceless

> When I interviewed White youth about how they identified racially, one boy said, "I don't know. I guess I'm just normal." When he said that, I saw myself in him. I know that when I was a teenager I didn't think of myself as White. I wouldn't have known then how to answer the very question I was now asking. —Ali

Most People of Color in the United States are taught from a young age that they have a race. Most White people are taught that they don't. Rather than see White as a race, most White people think about being White as being just "normal," as with the student in the example above.

HOW DO YOU IDENTIFY RACIALLY?

For people who were taught not to think much about their race, it can be particularly hard to learn that being White has meaning. Being seen for one's race first—before one's individuality, one's skills, one's talents, one's unique attributes—frankly, hurts. But that is precisely the experience that so many People of Color live with. This book is about building the stamina and capacity to engage with questions about race, which requires that every person see themselves as part of the racial puzzle of the US. It requires that everybody see not only how race impacts others, but how race impacts themselves. It requires that White people see that White, too, is a race.

Why does it matter if White people see themselves as White? It matters because the inability to do so is one of the biggest barriers to White people taking action against the racial hierarchy, against racism. White people tend to think of themselves as existing *outside* the racial dynamics of the US. The characters in the cartoon at the beginning of this chapter represent teenagers responding to a question that was asked of them in a study that Ali performed several years ago. Just like many White adults in our society, they struggled to identify as White when asked, "How do you identify racially?" Their difficulty makes sense because they identify with those parts of their ethnicity or lifestyles that give their lives meaning, and Whiteness is not something that gives them meaning, at least not meaning they are aware of.

Identifying as Irish, even if it's really just once or twice a year on holidays, is likely more meaningful to Irish Americans than their Whiteness is. Similarly, for someone who is an engineer, that identity resonates with their talents and training; Whiteness seems incidental to who they are. The problem is that even if Whiteness holds no conscious meaning for a person's identity, it is still critical to who they are and how they live their life. For most White people, their lives would be completely different if they were not White. It's hard to understand this if you don't understand how *not being White* impacts the lives of People of Color every day.

> As a Black woman, I have been aware of my race since I can remember. I picked up on comments that my parents made when we were in public, even as a child. I remember when I was about eleven years old

returning from a week at an environmental camp.
My mom and I went into a store shortly after she
picked me up. We had only a few items, so I told
the cashier that no bag would be necessary in my
attempt to keep one more plastic bag out of the
landfill and out of the ocean. My mom interrupted,
"Yes, we do need a bag and the receipt!" She let me
know when we got in the car that we always have to
ask cashiers to put our items in a bag and make sure
to carry a receipt. "Otherwise they will think you
stole it." I was young, but I knew who "they" were
right away. —Toni

What Is a Racial Hierarchy?

Every person who lives in the US lives within a racial hierarchy. This term refers to the way that racial groups have historically been assigned different value, literally ranked according to which ones are seen as more or less deserving of resources. Historian Isabel Wilkerson uses the term "racial caste system" to describe this phenomenon.

In the US, those who are seen as "White" have always been positioned by laws, policies, and even informal interactions at the top of this hierarchy, while those who are seen as "Black" have always been positioned by the system at the bottom. As Isabel Wilkerson has written, "While the requirements to qualify as white have changed over the centuries, the fact of a dominant caste has remained constant from its inception—whoever fit the definition of white, at whatever

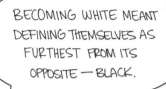

Isabel Wilkerson is a journalist and writer who was the first Black woman to receive a Pulitzer Prize in journalism.[1] She gained fame with her book *The Warmth of Other Suns*—a history book that reads like a novel. It is the story of the Great Migration of Black Americans from the Jim Crow South to the northern and western regions of the country. Her best-selling book *Caste: The Origins of Our Discontents* (from 2020) explains the system of racism in the United States as similar in form to the caste system in India.

point in history, was granted the legal rights and privileges of the dominant caste."[3]

How does the racial hierarchy stay in place? It is held up by many different social forces, some of which are so big and so pervasive (like public policy) that we might not even recognize them, just as we don't recognize the networks of pipes that bring water to our homes. Other social forces (like blatant stereotypes in movies) are specific enough that we might recognize them in our everyday lives if we are paying attention. No aspect of our society is exempt from these forces. Here is a list of some of the social forces that fortify the racial hierarchy:

Narrow/Repetitive Media Representations of People of Color

People of Color are often cast in the same types of roles over and over again in movies and TV shows. They are often portrayed as violent, oversexualized, and angry, or they (and their cultural styles or ways of talking) are used as a source of humor. At the same time, White people have many more choices in their roles—for example, as the hero, an innocent and willing object of sexual conquest (for women), a character rooted in a strong nuclear family, or a smart person.[4] If White people commit violence in movies, it is almost always justified as being necessary to the plot. Even when White people are depicted as evil, there are so many other roles available for White people that viewers don't see that one evil person as representing all White people.

In movies and TV, Black people are often portrayed as angry and as violent in ways that are unnecessarily and inexplicably destructive. Asian Americans are regularly depicted as the desexualized computer nerd (for men) and the exotic, oversexualized, quiet one (for women). Latinx characters are often portrayed as loving to dance, having a Spanish accent, being very emotional, and hyperromantic. Native American figures—time and again—are portrayed as being either nature loving or intoxicated. These common stereotypical representations reinforce the racial hierarchy because they lend credence to the idea that White people are better, more responsible, and more capable of serving the common good. They reinforce the idea that People of Color are somehow dysfunctional and therefore deserve a lower rank in the racial hierarchy.

Segregated Neighborhoods and Schools

Based on decades of policies in which the federal government invested only in segregated housing and refused to invest in integrated communities,[5] most neighborhoods and communities in the US are racially segregated, as are most schools. This segregation impacts the racial realities of White children and teens, who tend to perceive that they live in a mostly White world, one populated with very few People of Color (even though there are actually more People of Color in the world than White people).

Segregated neighborhoods and schools reinforce the racial hierarchy because they keep people separate. When we are separate from one another, we don't know one another's realities, we don't build relationships with each other, we don't have as much empathy for each other. We develop different cultural references and even different slang, which makes it hard to connect and relate. On top of that, our society tends to see Black slang as inferior to White slang, which means that assumptions about Black inferiority (and White superiority) get in the way of connecting as well.

When we live in segregated communities, people begin to see racial groups almost as teams, or as groups defined by nature. People will say, "Like attracts like." Or, "In the same way that robins mate with other robins—not with eagles or hummingbirds—people should stay with people who are like them." In reality, there is no natural, biological distinction between people of different racial groups. We are not naturally separate groups like species of birds, but rather have been separated *into* groups by laws, policies, and practices that enforced separation, using categories of race that were made up. Segregation in neighborhoods and schools reinforces the false idea that racial separation is natural, comfortable, and preferable, when in fact it has been intentionally created and enforced, in both explicit and implicit ways. Over time, it comes to *appear* to be natural. This upholds the racial hierarchy.

Depiction of White People as the Human Ideal

Rather than seeing people of all different racial backgrounds as worthy and capable, our society tends to see White ways of doing things (White ways of talking, of walking, of dressing, of naming children) as ideal or even as "normal," while People of Color are often seen as a deviation from that norm, as "different," "weird," and "less than."

This idealization of White styles reinforces the racial hierarchy because it affirms the notion that White people deserve to be at the top. It suggests that the ranking exists for good reason, and in fact that White people—and the way White people do things—actually *are* better. People of Color have always found ways to challenge this framing, to celebrate their uniqueness and embrace aspects of their identities that have been denigrated by the White mainstream. Check out the link to this video performed by three slam poets titled "Unforgettable," where they lift up the beauty of names for People of Color.[6]

Truncated History

In most schools, students do not learn a full, complete, or even accurate history of the United States. Most Americans do not realize that George Washington enslaved African people, even when he was president, or that Thomas Jefferson, who famously wrote that "all men are created equal," enslaved hundreds of African people. If we don't learn the history of racial oppression, how can we understand how it has shaped the racial reality that we currently live in? The racial hierarchy appears to be natural when we don't learn about the laws and policies that limited opportunities for People of Color while benefiting and advancing White people. Not fully understanding our history makes it very hard to understand why there is consistent inequality in life outcomes and why that is a problem. When people don't understand racism it's often because they haven't been taught certain fundamental aspects of US history.

Stop and take a look at all the ways that we receive information when we are in school. Most of what we learn comes from White teachers (after all, 79 percent of the teachers in the US are White).[7] Most of what we learn is about White people. Most of our books and curricular materials were created by White people. When we learn about people who are not White, it is often during a special section of the curriculum or a specific time of the year. What this means is that we come to see White people and White lives as the default, the most prevalent, or the most important to learn about.

> *Growing up, I had a Black teacher almost every year from pre-K until fifth grade. While it was great to have teachers that were reflections of me, our curriculum was not. My favorite author was Beverly Cleary. Cleary's books featured characters like Ramona, a White girl with red hair, and her older sister, Beezus. Besides Black History Month, I remember learning mostly about White people. When we did study someone that wasn't White, it was always a big deal. We named and celebrated Black authors because they were Black. But when the authors were White, nobody said anything about their Whiteness. —Toni*

Ideologies of Meritocracy and Individualism

Meritocracy is the idea that if you work hard, you will get ahead, and the only thing that keeps you from not getting ahead is that you are not working hard enough. This belief is common in the United States. Big beliefs that are common across a culture—so common that they are hard to question or doubt—are called *ideologies*. The ideology of meritocracy supports the racial hierarchy because it claims that each individual person is responsible for their own success or failure. It ignores how a person's opportunities, access to resources, education, jobs, and social networks have been shaped by race and by their other group memberships, such as class and gender.

The ideology of meritocracy leads to the ideology of individualism. If each person is solely responsible for their own success or failure, then everything is up to the individual. The ideology goes like this: if they fail it's their fault; if they succeed, it's because of who they are and how hard they worked. Think about it this way: two students get into an Ivy League college. One of them can't go because her parents don't have the money, and the other is able to attend debt-free. Does attending that college make the second student better, smarter, more accomplished? Student #1 is not less capable or meritorious than Student #2, but she may be unable to access the same opportunities in spite of her merits. The ideology of meritocracy is a myth because it erases the power that laws, systems, and history have over people's lives, opportunities, and success or failure. Individualism also suggests that every individual thinks for themselves, that they come to their ideas freely and without outside influence. Individualism ignores the fact that we are all part of a collective culture that trains us to think and believe in similar ways. How does culture teach us what to believe? Take gender, for example: gender-reveal parties, toy manufacturers, and clothing companies promote the idea that blue is for boys and pink is for girls. The symbolism of these two colors is known and often used throughout US society, even though most of us know that children don't come in shades of blue and pink. Similarly, boys often get the message that they should be tough or that they should not be emotionally vulnerable, while girls are often encouraged to care about their appearance. These ways of thinking are enforced by family, media, and our culture at large. It makes being wholly "individual" extremely hard.

What do individualism and meritocracy have to do with racism? The ideology of individualism reinforces the racial hierarchy because it suggests that all our thoughts are independently generated—that each person comes up with their own unique ideas with no influence from the rest of society. This erases the reality that we absorb messages about people of different racial groups (and our own racial groups) on a daily basis. The myth of meritocracy reinforces the racial hierarchy because it allows people to believe that those who have more deserve more because they must have worked for it. It suggests that people who are poor deserve to be poor because they would have more if they worked harder. It erases the historical and political context that actively denied opportunities for People of Color while creating opportunities for White people to save money, get educated, work, and build wealth.

We can also see individualism as an ideology that underlies climate change. The more we see our individual actions as independent and separate from those around us, the less likely we are to recognize our collective impact on one another and on the Earth. Taking action on climate change requires us to recognize our interconnection and interdependence with one another—and with people across the globe whom we have yet to meet. Climate change is a collective problem. The solutions that work will be collective solutions.

Socialization

> **Socialization** is the process of being taught or trained to behave correctly within your culture and to see the world as your culture teaches you to see it.
>
> DEFINITION

One thing White people have in common is their racial socialization. White people are socialized *as White people* by society—through parents, neighborhoods, schools, geography, friends, music, movies, and so on. In turn, White people have similar patterns of response to the same racialized events, even if they grew up in different neighborhoods and went to different schools. See if you can predict likely reactions to the following events:

1. Four contestants on *Survivor* bond together to form a Black alliance. How does the predominantly White viewership respond?
2. A Black woman dies in police custody. What do you see in the comments section of Instagram?
3. An Asian American student gets into an Ivy League college. What do your White peers say?

Answer key:

1. "I just want to watch my show. Why do they have to focus on race?" "They're discriminating against White people!"
2. "I wonder what she did. Everyone knows you should comply with police."
3. "Of course they would get in. All they do is study." "It's because they have tiger moms."

How did you do? Even if you only got one out of three, you know something about White racial socialization. The responses to some of these statements are predictable because so many people receive a similar socialization. White people tend to be taught:

- not to see or talk about race (to be colorblind)
- to not be "racist"—which means to avoid expressing overt racism in the form of racial slurs or intentional discrimination, at least not in front of People of Color
- to believe in meritocracy and individualism

It is rare that White people are taught to be anti-racist or taught how to counter racist humor. White people in the US tend to be socialized to see individuals as responsible for their own fate, rather than to see the ways in which people are impacted by the system. When White people respond to racism or racial ideas in the same ways over and over again, it is because of their common socialization.

Yeah, but... **I would interrupt that racism, and I'm White.**

If you are White and you feel that this socialization doesn't describe you, that's okay. There are definitely exceptions to every rule. But even if you were socialized to be anti-racist, the chances are good that these responses are still familiar to you. As you read, we encourage you to think about how White racial socialization impacts you, even if it doesn't describe you perfectly or in all cases.

What Is White Fragility?

The phrase "white fragility" describes a common reaction among White people when their ideas about racism are challenged. That typical reaction is defensiveness, often in the form of anger or hurt. This defensiveness is the result of living at the top of a racial hierarchy that society teaches us either does not exist or is a natural outcome due to true differences between racial groups. Because White people are socialized not to see or acknowledge racism, discussions that challenge the racial hierarchy often provoke deep defensiveness in people who have been taught to see US society as fair and open to anyone who works hard. White fragility, as we will explore in the rest of the book, is a block to learning about racism, challenging the hierarchy, and connecting with People of Color.

Privilege: The Word Everyone Loves to Hate

Because of the racial hierarchy, it is literally less safe to be a Person of Color than to be a White person. This means that most People of Color are aware of the racial hierarchy—and of racism—because they *need* to be aware of it in order to keep themselves safe as they navigate their lives. White people, by and large, do not need to be aware of their Whiteness in order to survive and even thrive. This is called privilege.

"Privilege" is a term that can be hard for people to understand. Sometimes White people hear the term and think, "I don't live in a huge house. I don't have a ton of spare cash. How can I have privilege?" Privilege doesn't mean that a person is rich or that they have everything they want. Privilege means getting to live without the inconvenience, pain, and structural barriers of a particular kind of discrimination. The kind of discrimination this book addresses is racial. White people may face barriers, but racism is not one of them. Ironically, privilege feels like "being normal." It feels like being free. Another way to say a person has privilege is to say they are in a social group that doesn't *dis*advantage them.

Being in the White mainstream means that White people are often unaware of what People of Color experience in US society. White people don't have to understand the experiences of People of Color in order to survive, whereas People of Color need to know the rules of Whiteness in order to survive and succeed. For example, many Black men learn early that wearing workout clothes, including a hoodie, might mean that people take them less seriously, fear them, or will even threaten their lives because they assume that a Black man in a hoodie is dangerous. Many Black men might wear a suit and tie or a nice dress shirt to events where White men would dress casually. Ironically, White people don't necessarily have to follow the rules of Whiteness to be safe. Simply being White often satisfies that requirement.

What makes racism and other types of oppression so powerful is that they are backed by the government and other influential institutions. The battle for women's suffrage is a clear example. Women in the US did not get the right to vote (suffrage) until 1920, and there was only one possible way they could obtain that right: men had to give it to them. Women couldn't grant it to themselves, they couldn't vote on it, and they couldn't even openly advocate for it because they weren't allowed to speak in many public places. Only men could grant women their civil rights. So while women could be prejudiced against men and be mean to a man in a one-on-one interaction, women as a group couldn't literally deny every single man in the society his civil rights. But men as a group *could* deny every single woman in society hers. If they are both prejudiced, what was the difference? His prejudice was backed by the government and its laws—which his group controlled—and hers wasn't.

Now imagine a man from that era who believed that all people should have the right to vote, and he worked hard to make that happen. His advocacy would have had a big impact because he was from a group with social power. But he also still benefitted from the reality that women couldn't vote, whether he agreed that they should be able to or not; he was still *automatically privileged* by his society. He was part of a group (White men) whose voices and ideas mattered even more because they could vote in a society where very few people could. Even if he protested by refusing to vote until all people had the right, he still had that choice to make, when women and People of Color did not. He didn't lose his privilege just because he was against having it. You don't have to want or exercise privilege to get it—society automatically grants it to you. The question is how you use it to undo the very structures that gave it to you in the first place.

Historical note: Although most history books tell us that women received the right to vote in 1920, it was actually *White* women who got that right, and it was granted to them by *White* men. *All* women did not gain full access until passage of the Voting Rights Act of 1965. Although technically the US Constitution allowed people of all races to legally vote before passage of this act, in reality some states prevented Black people from doing so by imposing literacy tests or poll taxes. In other words, it took the passage of a separate law to enforce a right supposedly guaranteed in the US Constitution. This is an example of how the experiences of White people are held up as if they represent everyone's experiences. This is what it means to tell history from a White perspective.

Dominant Fragility

Most people have at least one dominant group membership that automatically grants them privilege.[8] Besides being White, these memberships include being heterosexual, being a citizen of the US, being cisgender, being a man, being non-disabled, being Christian, and being middle class or wealthy.

Being in a dominant group means that—at least in terms of that part of your identity—you are in the social mainstream. If you are part of the heterosexual mainstream, for example, you probably didn't have a big process of coming out to family and friends. You didn't have to fight for decades to gain the right to marry the person of your choice or live in fear that every time that right gets challenged in court, it could be taken away. Heterosexual people feel "just normal" and go through life without really questioning social norms and privileges

DID JACKIE ROBINSON REALLY BREAK THE COLOR LINE?

Another example of White people having the power to grant access to others (and take it away) is the story of Jackie Robinson. Robinson is often celebrated as the first African American to break the color line and play in major-league baseball. While Robinson was certainly an amazing baseball player, this story line depicts him as *racially* special, a Black man who broke the color barrier all by himself. The message is that Robinson finally had what it took to play with White people, as if no Black athlete before him was talented enough to compete at that level. Imagine if instead the story went something like this: "Jackie Robinson was the first Black man that White people allowed to play major-league baseball." This version makes an important distinction, because no matter how fantastic a player Robinson was, he simply could not play in the major leagues if White people—who controlled the institution—did not allow it. Had he walked onto the field before being granted permission to by White owners and policy makers, the police would have removed him. The way we usually tell this story hides the fact that, historically, White people had the power to make the rules. Stories told this way also do White people a disservice by failing to show us the White allies who, behind the scenes, worked hard and long to open the field to African American players. These allies could serve as much-needed role models for other White people.

based on their sexual identity. The social assumption is that if you are not heterosexual, you will figure that out and let people know, and if you don't have equal rights, you will be the one to have to fight for them. If you are nondisabled, you probably have very little awareness of whether your school or workplace is accessible to disabled people.[9] You may never even have stopped to think about whether a person who cannot go up and down stairs could enter your building. You may never have thought about the fact that you don't have disabilities. You just don't have them. If you don't struggle with mental illness, then you probably have never considered the inner conflict many people go through concerning how much to disclose about their mental illness to peers and coworkers, even when their condition does not affect their school or work performance. One feature of having a dominant identity is that you often don't realize the vulnerability, invalidation, and even violence that people experience by virtue of not being a part of that dominant group. Another is that you are usually unaware of how being a part of that dominant group gives you social power and protection.

This is a book about white fragility. But if we broadened the scope, we could call it "dominant fragility."[10] Anyone with a dominant identity (which, again, is most of us, whether we are nondisabled, men, cisgender, heterosexual, middle class/wealthy, White, Christian, or have a normative body type) is likely to demonstrate some fragility when learning about that identity and the unfair advantage it automatically grants us. The idea of white fragility can be expanded to help us describe the defensive behaviors and maneuvers employed by any member of a dominant group when learning that they are not "just normal." In reality, they are positioned at the top of a hierarchy that they didn't design and they didn't ask for but that still benefits them at the expense of others. As you read this book, we invite you to consider how the concept of fragility—and how to challenge it—can be expanded in your own life and practice, regardless of your racial background. In other words, if you are a Person of Color and you identify as heterosexual, we invite you to consider what privileges come with that—and how heterosexual fragility might manifest for you when your advantages are challenged. If you are a Person of Color and you are nondisabled or cisgender, we invite you to think about how those identities privilege you.

The point of learning about privilege or dominant identities is not to help us see how lucky we are or how we take for granted advantages that we should be grateful for. It is not to make us feel ashamed or guilty. Understanding privilege is about seeing where we are located in an unjust system in which we unwittingly benefit from others' oppression. It's about working to change that system. And it's also about seeing how the lenses we use to view the world are shaped by our dominant identities.

> *If I've only ever been treated well by police officers because I'm both White and gender conforming as a cisgender woman, it's going to be hard for me to understand the reality of someone who has only ever been questioned, scrutinized, and intimidated by police officers, as many People of Color, trans people, and gender nonconforming people have been. I can't change the fact that there are realities I don't automatically have access to in my own experiences. But if I realize that my lens is shaped by my dominant identities—and if I listen to people with lenses that are different from my own—then I will have a much fuller view of racism and oppression. And I will have a better sense of how I can use my access and privilege to change the system. —Ali*

In this chapter, we talked about why race can be so hard for White people to understand. It gets easier when White people figure out what it means to be White within a racial hierarchy. Once a person can see their Whiteness and see the racial hierarchy, it's hard to unsee it. And it starts to make sense why they didn't see it before. The racial hierarchy itself keeps racial groups separate. White people often don't have exposure to the lenses and points of view of peers and colleagues who fall elsewhere on the hierarchy. Once a person can see those dynamics, it becomes clear how important it is to listen to and connect with people who have a different vantage point based on their own racial positions. As we will learn throughout this book, white fragility makes it almost impossible to listen and connect across race. That is why it matters so much that we understand what it is—and what we can do about it.

Afterthoughts

DISCUSSION

With a small group of people, discuss how the following statements might stop a conversation about racism:

- "I was taught to treat everyone the same."
- "People just need to be taught to respect one another, and that begins at home."
- "It's horrible that an innocent Black man was killed, but destroying property has to stop."

Journal

What conversations might be hard for you as you read this book?

Chapter 2

RACISM, SUPREMACISTS, SUPREMACY

Until I was twenty years old, I did not really know what racism was. I had been taught that racism was intentional hatred and violence directed at people because of their skin color. I thought that "racists" were people who used the n-word and who joined the KKK. Racists—as far as I knew—were proud of being racists. I mistakenly thought that most of the racists lived in the South and generally held working-class jobs. Given that I didn't fall into those categories, and I wasn't a card-carrying member of any racist clubs, I figured I could not be racist. I figured racism had nothing to do with me. —Ali

Racism Is Bigger Than the KKK

Ali's story about how she learned *who is a racist* is common. Many people learn that racists are mean people who intentionally want to do harm to people of other races. And for that reason, most people are against racism. But this incorrect idea is precisely why racism is so hard to address. Most of us are missing the main point. If racism were just an individual problem of meanness, it would be much easier to confront. But in fact, racism is a *system*. It is a system in the US in which people are divided into racial boxes. Since the very first days of nationhood—and even before—resources and opportunities have been distributed to people depending on what box they are put in. And, as this chapter will show, White people have always been in the box that is given the largest shares of both.

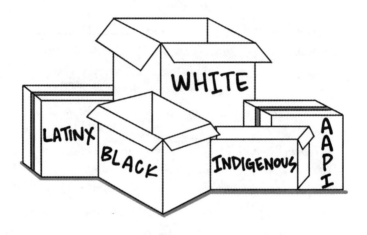

Another common misconception about racism is this: "As long as I'm not racist, I'm good." In fact, psychologist Dr. Beverly Daniel Tatum proposes that racism operates more like one of those moving walkways at the airport.[1] If you are standing on the moving walkway, you don't even have to move—you will be carried by it. Standing still in a society that has been shaped by systemic racism means that White people will be impacted by—and benefit from—systemic racism *without doing anything*. The only way to actively resist racism is to walk *the wrong way* on the moving walkway. It's awkward and difficult to move against the flow. And yet that is how we make change.

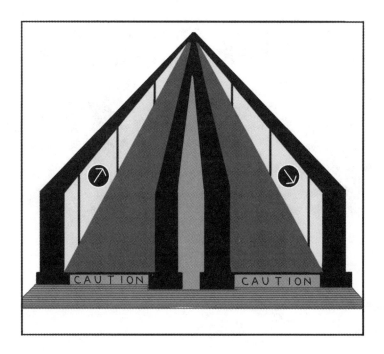

There is good news and bad news here. The bad news is
that racism is everywhere. It's not just one person or group
of people. It's baked into our laws, our institutions, even
our culture. The good news is, because racism is a system—
because it is *systemic*—and we are inside this system, then
any one of us can take anti-racist action. We can choose to
move against the flow of the moving walkway and confront a
system that was designed to divide us from one another and
treat us unequally.

What Does It Mean to Say That Racism Is Systemic?

In order to understand the concept of systemic racism,
we have to establish what a system is. A system is a set of

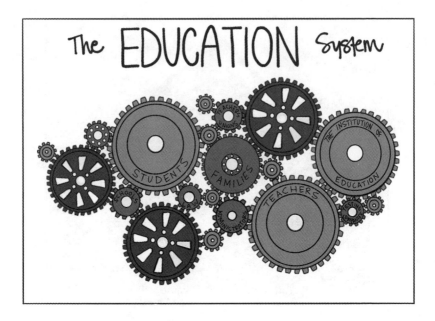

The EDUCATION System

interrelated parts. These parts include individuals, groups
of people, organizations, ideas, institutions, and more.
Education, for example, is an institution comprising many
parts: students, schools, teachers, administrators, parent-
teacher associations, textbook writers and publishers, teachers' unions, families, education law, testing companies, etc.
Systemic racism means that racism is built into all parts of
society. The institution of *education,* together with other
institutions, like *medicine, science,* and *law,* together form the
system of our society.

We are going to look briefly at how two institutions in
particular were used to create and justify racism: science and
the law.

How "Science" Helped Justify Unequal Treatment of Races

I remember growing up and seeing pictures of slavery. How could a human treat another human being with such cruelty? —Toni

When we look back today at the American system of enslavement, it's hard to imagine anyone thinking it was a good idea. Of course, there were many people who knew it was a terrible idea, namely the enslaved people and the few White allies who stood up against their enslavement. But for those whose financial fortunes depended on using the free labor of enslaved Africans, there needed to be a way to convince the general voting public (which at that time included only White, land-owning men) that supporting slavery was not cruel or unusual.

What if they could prove that enslaved Africans were not harmed by enslavement? What if they could demonstrate that enslaved Africans were better off in families that had been separated, under the violent control of White overseers, and enslaved for all their lives and all their children's and grandchildren's lives, for generation after generation? It wouldn't be easy, but what if they could prove that enslaved Africans were actually less than human, and that they benefited from the control of a superior group of people? What if science said it were true?

Thomas Jefferson, the nation's third president and the owner of over six hundred enslaved Africans,[2] was one of scores of politicians and scientists who advanced the idea that Black people were inferior so that they could justify enslavement. Politicians worked with scientists to prove the theory that there are natural, biological differences between races. They were interested in justifying a racial hierarchy that declared White people a separate and distinct "racial" group from Black people. Scientists set out to prove that White people were biologically programmed to be more intelligent than Black people, while Black people were more biologically suited to physical labor. Using head size, body type, and other measures that we know today are arbitrary and ridiculous, Jefferson and many scientists laid out a framework for racial differences that dehumanized enslaved Africans and justified their treatment under slavery.

This was the beginning of what is called scientific racism. Scientific racism was used to justify the unequal treatment not only of enslaved Africans, but of Indigenous people and Mexican people as well. The US economy, in fact, was based on the abduction and enslavement of African people, the displacement, land theft, and genocide of Indigenous people, and the annexation of Mexican lands. The everyday White citizen would more readily sign off on these actions if they could be convinced that the actions were good for the people in those groups, or that people in those groups were incapable of self-government—or even self-control—to begin with. White people would also be less likely to resist if they benefited in some way from the arrangement.

While a defining feature of science in the twenty-first century is the scientific method, which helps scientists to be more objective in their work, science is not and has never been neutral. The answers that science gives us depend, in large part, on the questions we ask. In Jefferson's day, the late 1700s and early 1800s, the questions people asked already assumed the answers they sought. Scientists didn't ask, "*Are* Blacks (and others) inferior?" They asked, "*Why are* Blacks (and others) inferior?" You can see how this question assumed that the inferiority of Black people was a given, and the scientists' task was only to show why. The starting point was problematic because it assumed inferiority. Scientists were looking for ways to validate a theory they already held, a theory that was politically useful for them, a theory that justified the unequal treatment required to maintain the wealth and control of an elite White few.

Race itself isn't actually real. What we know today is that there is no biological difference between people of different skin colors, except the fact that they have developed different amounts of melanin in their bodies as they adapted to their environments over time. Skin colors are different, and that is real. But being put in the White or Black or AAPI (Asian American/Pacific Islander) or Latinx or Native box does not make a person more or less intelligent, more or less athletic, more or less qualified for a certain type of work or education. What "race" a person is depends on what box they were put into, and then how the group in that box was treated by the government and society. If White people demonstrated higher aptitude in the educational system, it wasn't because they were inherently more intelligent; it was because the government, for much of US history, and even today, has made it more difficult for people who are not White to access quality schooling.

At the risk of repeating ourselves, we'll say that again. Differences that we see with our eyes, like skin color, eye shape, and hair texture, are real. The values and beliefs we attach to these differences are made up. Race is made up. The concept of race didn't even exist until there was a reason to separate people to justify exploiting them.

Yeah, but... **if race is made up, why do we have to keep talking about it?**

Race is a fiction. But racism is real. And it has a huge impact on people's lives. We need to keep talking about it so that we can work to create a society in which racism does not impact a person's life chances or outcomes. We talk about it so that we can recognize and dismantle the racial hierarchy.

> **Racism** is one group's collective racial prejudice and discrimination backed with power. Because the group with power controls the institutions of society, its prejudice becomes infused across the society and reproduces itself automatically. In the US and other Western-oriented societies, White people control the institutions, and racism works to their benefit at the expense of People of Color. Racism operates at the individual, group, and system levels.
>
> **DEFINITION**

Ta-Nehisi Coates writes, "But race is the child of racism, not the father."[3] Many people think that race came first. But actually, race and racial groupings are a product of racism, and of the need to dehumanize certain groups so as to more expediently and cheaply take their labor or their land. People were exploited first, and then race and racial difference were created to justify that exploitation.

Ta-Nehisi Coates is a Black journalist and writer. He first gained popularity with articles he wrote about race and racism in *The Atlantic*. His book *Between the World and Me* was a *New York Times* best seller in 2015. The book is written as a letter to his son about the struggles and joys of being Black in America. Toni Morrison said of Coates, "I've been wondering who might fill the intellectual void that plagued me after James Baldwin died. Clearly it is Ta-Nehisi Coates."[4]

How the Law Was Used to Decide
Who Got to Be White

My ancestors came to the US from England, Germany, Scotland, and Denmark. I don't know much about my European ancestry because they came to the US so long ago that most of their connections to Europe are lost to the generations. I imagine that life was challenging for them, and I am sure that they worked hard. But I know for certain that as Western Europeans, my ancestors immigrated to the US and were able to become citizens and enjoy the full benefits of citizenship, because they were White. And I wonder sometimes if they had any idea how much easier their lives were than people who were not considered White? —Ali

Who is White? This is a question that has been asked repeatedly throughout US history because the stakes connected to the answer are incredibly high. When the term "white" first appeared in colonial law in the late 1600s, being "white" meant that a person could not be owned by other human beings. It meant that they owned themselves and their children. It meant that they could own property, and that included owning other human beings. By 1790, one's "race" was becoming part of how people thought about themselves, and Whiteness was the only named racial category. When the US census began asking people to report their race, the options included:[5]

- free white males
- free white females
- all other free persons
- slaves

The US government also needed a way to determine who was and was not "Indian" or Native American. By 1825 the government started using "blood quantum," or perceived degree of "Indian blood" in a person's body, to determine who would be classified as "Indian." The common misperception was that one could have "White blood" or "Black blood" or "Indian blood," and that even one drop of "Black blood" or "Indian blood" meant that a person could not be White. Of course this idea is scientifically absurd, but it was effective in protecting the idea of White racial "purity." For that reason, all the children born to enslaved Black women as the result of being raped by White men were seen as "Black," even though in today's terms they would be considered "mixed" or "multiracial." We know now that there's no such thing as "Black blood" or "White blood" and that all human beings descend from a common ancestor. We know that the effort to quantify one's race was connected to the need to maintain a distinct separation between racial groups so that the dominant group (White people) could continue to control material resources. In this case, the material resources that were under dispute were land, otherwise occupied by Indigenous people, as well as the bodies and labor of Black people, which should have belonged exclusively to the Black people themselves.

Did you know that in some cases, people didn't know if they were White? Perhaps they thought they were White, or wanted to be White, but people in their town said otherwise. Because citizenship in the US was tied to Whiteness, and because land ownership was tied to citizenship, those people needed to be legally recognized as White in order to start businesses, own land, vote, contribute to making law, and receive all the protections of US citizenship status, including carrying a passport.

Between 1878 and 1952, there were fifty-two cases in which people went to court to ask the courts to declare them "White."[6] This wasn't because they thought it would be nice to be a different race. It was because Whiteness brought with it the full benefits and protections of citizenship that were unavailable to them otherwise; White privilege was actually set in law! The people who filed racial prerequisite cases were very clear that they would have a better chance of building their hopes and dreams if the legal system classified them as White. They could reap the rewards of their hard work rather than working every day of their lives without ever being able to own the land they tilled or the shops they ran.

During those years (1878–1952), people who were Chinese, Japanese, Asian Indian, Syrian, Mexican, Native American, Punjabi, Armenian, and multiracial went to court to argue for their Whiteness. Sometimes the courts found them to be White, sometimes not. The courts relied on the belief that racial groups were real and distinct to make decisions about who was or wasn't White. Most people believed that race itself was real and unchangeable, but clearly some people didn't believe this, or they wouldn't think it possible to challenge their racial designation in court.

The argument that the courts used to declare or deny a plaintiff's Whiteness is one of the most mind bending. The judge in one case literally said, "A white person is a person the average, well-informed white person knows to be white."[7] What this means is that White people get to decide who is White. Basically, you know one when you see one . . . if you are one.

THE KKK AND THE POWER OF YOUTH

Several groups today still believe in and promote the idea that all human beings belong to biologically distinct racial groups. Formerly known as White Supremacists or the KKK, these groups now call themselves the alt-right or White Nationalists. (The groups QAnon and the Proud Boys also fall into this general category.) They shifted from identifying as "White Supremacists" to "White Nationalists" in order to make white supremacy seem more normal, more acceptable, less Nazi-ish.

One of the people behind this rebranding was a White teen named Derek Black.[8] Derek was raised in Florida and homeschooled by his parents, both of whom identified as White Supremacists. David Duke, a leader of the KKK, was his godfather. Even as a young teen, Derek could see that the old-fashioned racism of the KKK was not going to be mainstream anytime soon, and he worked with his parents and godfather to rebrand White Supremacist ideology to make it more attractive to more average White people. They could do this by calling it White Nationalism and by suggesting that they weren't really interested in hurting Black people or People of Color in general, but more in preserving White racial purity. According to Derek, they were about protecting and promoting White people, not hurting anybody else.

As a youth, Derek designed a White Supremacist web platform for young people, based on Stormfront, the adult White Supremacist platform that his father ran. He and his father also maintained a listserve for people who

(*continued*)

wanted to be part of Stormfront. But they had a problem: they only wanted White people to be a part of the list-serve. How could they decide, given that they were trying to accommodate tens of thousands of anonymous users, who was and was not White? Did it matter how dark their skin was? Could multiracial people become members? What about immigrants from Poland? From Russia? From Australia? Were they White? Ultimately, Stormfront did the same thing that the US judicial system did in 1920. They decided that if another White person who was a member of Stormfront could vouch for someone's Whiteness, then that person could join the listserve. Sound familiar? "A white person is a person the average, well-informed white person knows to be white."

The work of Derek Black has had an enormous impact on US government and society. He himself has said that he believes his work of rebranding and mainstreaming White Nationalism played a large role in the 2016 election and making mainstream racism such a central feature of Donald Trump's popular appeal. But he doesn't claim this notoriety with pride. Derek actually rescinded all his work in the White Supremacist movement after going to college, studying history, and making friends with people from other races. He realized that he had been taught inaccuracies and falsehoods by his family throughout his life. The more he learned about history and modern science, the more he could see that his White Supremacist ideology didn't actually hold up. In college, he studied the

(continued)

history of medieval Europe and began to see the roots of racial ideology and how it was constructed over time. He began to realize that a central tenet of White Supremacist ideology—that people belong to separate and distinct biological racial groups, and that some of those groups are better than others—was a lie. In addition to what he learned in classes, his classmates at his college began to recognize him as the face of the youth movement for White Nationalism. While many classmates shunned him or tried to get him kicked out of school, several took it on themselves to call him in, befriend him, engage him in conversation—and challenge him on his beliefs and actions. This small group of friends completely transformed his understanding of race, history, and the racial hierarchy that he had believed in so deeply. He began to understand that race is a social fiction.

Today Derek spends his time speaking and writing, trying to undo the damage he has done. But his story demonstrates something powerful. Young people are capable of making a huge difference. Derek was able to mobilize and transform an international movement based on his ideas, passion, and organizing prowess. Imagine what might have been possible if he had learned the truth about race and racism at a young age. Imagine what could have been possible with an anti-racist lens, rather than a racist one. Also consider the powerful impact the friends who didn't give up on him had on helping him change his views.

(continued)

Derek's story is hopeful, but he is just one person. There is so much more to be done. White Nationalism—the belief that our country should be run by and for Whites—is on the rise both in the United States and globally.

- While aspects of White Nationalism have existed for a long time, between 2016 and 2018 there was a major increase in activism by far-right groups.[9]
- In 2019, the number of White Nationalist groups rose for the second straight year—a 55 percent increase since 2017.[10]
- These groups include White Nationalists, neo-Nazis, Klansmen, and members of the so-called alt-right.
- The more radical groups want to start a race war through violence.[11]

The internet is a powerful recruitment tool for White Nationalists, and they especially target White teen boys. The founder and editor of a major neo-Nazi website has openly stated that they aim to influence boys as young as eleven, declaring, "My site is mainly designed to target children."[12] This is a powerful reminder of why we have to pay attention to our sources on social media (we'll say more about this topic in Chapter 9). Even though it can be disturbing to know about the harmful use of social media, we hope it is also empowering to know that there are things you can do to resist and to protect yourself. And each of us is needed.

The Impact of Overlapping Institutions

Understanding the systemic nature of racism is foundational to understanding why none of us can be outside of it. Feminist Marilyn Frye uses the image of a birdcage to describe how institutions merge together to form a system that serves to trap people inside. This intersection of institutions can be seen as a web or a network, but it can also be seen as a cage. Imagine a birdcage in which all the wires join together at the top to enclose the bird. If you look closely at one individual wire it seems relatively harmless. *Sure, not being able to vote means that you don't have a say in government, but what's the big deal? It's just one little action that takes place every few years.* But as you can see, the legal system intersects with the courts, with science, with ideology—all of which intersect with other institutions such as health, education, housing, etc., until ultimately every single aspect of life is impacted. When you look through the bars of a birdcage from up close, you only see the space between the bars, and the bird hardly seems captive. But when you step back, you can see the interlocking network

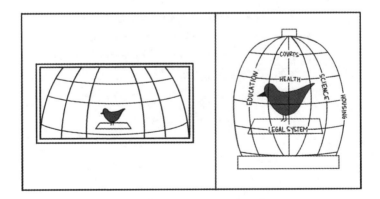

of bars and how they work together to make it very difficult to escape, especially since both the bird and its captors have been taught that the bird *belongs* in the cage.[13]

This is how systemic racism works. Systemic racism is the result of different institutions intersecting. Racism is not just the action of mean, prejudiced individuals. That's why good intentions or niceness doesn't make it go away. Racism is a system made up of many different institutions, beliefs, and practices.

I'm Definitely Not a White Supremacist!

When I first started learning about racism and White Supremacists, I could clearly distinguish myself from them. In fact, I liked to imagine that if I had lived in the 1960s, I would have stood up to the KKK and that I would have gone on the Freedom Rides, in which young people of all racial backgrounds registered Black voters in the Jim Crow South. But of course, I don't actually know what I would have done if I had lived during a time of such extreme, overt racial violence. As I get older I realize that unfortunately the KKK is only one small part of the problem. White supremacy is actually much bigger than White Supremacists. And it didn't end in the 1960s. It is still very much alive. —Ali

The term **Jim Crow South** refers to the laws and practices that legally segregated Black people from White people, primarily (but not exclusively) in the southern states of the US. Such practices included separate drinking fountains, prohibiting Black people from voting, and not allowing Black people to be in White neighborhoods after dark.

Question: What does it mean to say the US is a White Supremacist country?

This may be hard to accept, but after reading about how White people got sent to the front of the metaphorical line—for centuries—it's hard to deny that we live in a country that has historically put White people first. In this book, we refer to the US as a White Supremacist country. Not because we think the country is full of people who want to be in the KKK, but because our institutions (the wires coming together at the top of the birdcage) have prioritized White people above people of other racial backgrounds.

Using the phrase "White Supremacist" helps us name something that is usually invisible and unnamed. When we call it "white supremacy" and not just "racism," then it helps establish that it is not just a system that *disadvantages* Black people, Indigenous people, and People of Color. It is a system that simultaneously *advantages* White people. This means that White people have a foundational role in doing something about it.

If you are uncomfortable thinking about the US that way, or are having trouble answering the question we posed above, it's okay. Keep reading. Often when the language makes us uncomfortable, it's because we're not used to it or we don't understand some of the context behind it. We support you as you keep reading and stay open, even if you still have questions.

Prejudice Is Not Discrimination Is Not Racism

I remember meeting a man at a workshop. When I first saw him I saw a shaved head and combat boots, two triggers for me. Videos of neo-Nazis and White Supremacists with hair that matched his caused me to make a judgement about who he was before we even said a word to each other. Allowing myself the opportunity to get to know him and put those stereotypes to the side, I found out that he was a very kind and generous person. Had I not done that, I would never have known the beauty of who he really is. That can be a scary thing for me to do, especially as a Black woman whose history has taught me to be careful about trusting White people too quickly. —Toni

We don't want to spend too much time on vocabulary. Sometimes people can spend so much time debating the definition of racism that they never get around to actually doing something about it. At the same time, we need to talk about words so that we have some clarity around our meaning. And there are three terms that we think will be particularly useful to readers who want to be anti-racist, to travel the other way on the moving walkway.

The first word is prejudice. Prejudice is when we prejudge people based on something we think we know about them because of experiences with others in their group or even stereotypes we've seen in the media or heard from our families or friends. Everyone prejudges. It's not necessarily right or healthy, but it's normal and unavoidable.

The second word, discrimination, describes what we do when we take action based on our prejudices. For example, if a person has a prejudice against Black people because of a stereotype that they are not good at math, it will affect how they treat a Black classmate in a mandatory study group. They might grow impatient quickly, ignore their answers, fail to seek them out for help, or roll their eyes if they try to contribute. In other words, the way we see the world informs our actions. If a person has a prejudice that leads them to *treat* members of a certain racial group differently, they are discriminating. Just as everyone has prejudice, everyone discriminates in some way, often unconsciously and unintentionally. For example, disregarding and rolling your eyes at a classmate might be so automatic that you may not even realize you did it (but they likely noticed). Of course everyone has prejudice and discriminates, including Black people, and they may be rolling their eyes right back. But not everyone belongs to a group that has the power to enforce their prejudice in systematic ways. And this leads us to the third word: racism.

Racism is when a racial group's collective prejudice is backed by institutions and legal authority. Notice that in this definition, it's not actually about individual intentions at all. It's about having the power to implement your group's prejudice—even justify it—across all institutions. For example, as we have seen, White people had the power to enforce their prejudices against people who weren't White across all the laws and policies of US society; people who were not defined as White did not.

Sometimes people suggest that Black people are racist—for example, if an organization offers a scholarship designated specifically for Black people. If a scholarship is designated this way, the group funding the scholarship might be attempting to undo the impact of historical and systemic racism, which means that they have set aside money particularly for Black students. But we wouldn't call that racism because it's not an exclusion that is attempting to play into and uphold an entire web of institutions that exclude White people. In fact, it's the opposite. It's trying to rectify the exclusion of a group that has historically been left out.

Some White people call this reverse racism, as in: "That college is being reverse racist because they admitted a Latinx student and didn't admit me." The White student in this case assumed that the spot given to a Latinx student had been his. Had the college not prioritized admitting People of Color (the White student imagines) then he would have gotten in for sure. This kind of thinking is premised on the idea that all the spots at a given college were originally set aside for White people, and that whenever they are occupied by People of Color, they have somehow been taken from an otherwise deserving White person.

There are several problems with this logic. Can you see them?

The first has to do with the racial hierarchy. This thinking is rooted in an assumption that the racial hierarchy was and is legitimate, and that the first seats at a given college *should* be reserved for White students before anyone else.

The second problem with this thinking is that it ignores the fact that every college should have the prerogative to create an incoming class that will support all its students in having a rich academic experience. Overwhelming evidence shows that being part of a diverse class (diverse in background, racial perspective, academic interest, and worldview) makes students better at problem solving and teamwork.[14] Many colleges admit only about 10 percent of the tens of thousands of qualified applicants who apply. They try to construct classes of students who will enrich one another's learning and support the objectives of the college. Hopefully, they also work to challenge the assumptions of the racial hierarchy that historically dictated who got the first access to seats. Because this hierarchy has been proven to be illegitimate by major academic fields such as science, history, and sociology, it is in the interest of credible academic institutions to find ways to dismantle it.

The third problem with this thinking is that it assumes that Students of Color who are admitted are not *also* qualified, and that they could not be good enough to be admitted on their own merit.

The last problem with this assumption has to do with the actual state of affirmative action programs today. Although there were attempts throughout the latter half of the twentieth century to create more racial equity through affirmative action, most of those systems have been dismantled by challenges in the courts. So while it remains the right of most institutions to construct classes according to their values, most large universities no longer use race-based affirmative action programming to shape their admissions processes.

Accusations of "reverse racism" are intended to say that policies favoring Black, Latinx, and Indigenous people are racist toward White people. This accusation requires a belief that the racial hierarchy is the way things should be, that it's justified, that it's based on quantifiable differences between racial groups. But once we know the history of our country and the long legacy of racial inequality that underlies the current racial reality we see around us, we can begin to see the problems with assumptions based on the racial hierarchy. Some have called the reality of systemic racism three hundred years of affirmative action for White people!

We make many assumptions premised on the idea that the racial hierarchy is natural and legitimate. These assumptions lead us to see attempts to fix a racist legacy as racism toward White people. But once we eliminate the logic of the racial hierarchy, we can begin to understand the reasons we need programs like affirmative action to address historical wrongs.

Yeah, but… **Did affirmative action ever work?**

Ironically, affirmative action programming was most effective in achieving gender parity (not racial parity) in colleges and universities. White women are in fact the biggest beneficiaries of affirmative action in the twentieth century.[15] Although affirmative action was designed to address both racial and gender inequality, it was less effective at the former. Without a larger-scale project of helping people dismantle their assumptions embedded in the racial hierarchy, affirmative action programming in and of itself was constantly challenged in court. Think of the birdcage. University admissions was one bar that had been removed (or at least bent to the side), but the rest of the bars, including the courts, dominant racial ideology, and state law, served to put it back into place.

Here's one idea. Maybe we could reappropriate the term "reverse racism" as an anti-racist idea. If a college is attempting to *reverse* racism by *undoing* it, by rectifying historical wrongs, and by making sure that all students have an equitable chance to succeed, perhaps "reverse racism" is the right term. With that meaning, perhaps it holds water. You cannot accuse someone of reverse racism in the sense that "Your positive treatment of Black people makes you reverse racist toward White people," because we don't live in a system that has historically fostered racial equality. If we did, then attempts to advantage Black people, Indigenous people, and People of Color would be unfair to White people. But knowing the history of our country and the long legacy of racial inequality, one can begin to see why we need more institutions to engage in "reversing racism"—not by mistreating White people but by creating policies that tear down the racial hierarchy once and for all. In this case, "reverse" is better as a verb than an adjective.

Everyone holds prejudice and acts on it at times. And while racism privileges White people, this does not mean that individual White people do not struggle or face barriers. It simply means that White people do not face those barriers *because they are White*. Nor do they face racism *in addition to* other barriers they may face.

Racism is about multiple institutions coming together to create the overall system of racial inequality. Individual White people may be against racism, but they still benefit from a system that privileges White people as a group. This is not about good people or bad people. It's about systemic power and control. Being an anti-racist person means learning to see racism in the system around us, anticipating racism in ourselves, and working to change it in both. The chart below illustrates just a few of the institutions that White people control.

TOP DECISION MAKERS IN...

CONGRESS

MILITARY

WHITE HOUSE

CLASSROOMS

COLLEGES

TELEVISION

MOVIES

BOOKS

NEWS

MUSIC

Afterthoughts

DISCUSSION

- Presidency: 99% White
- Vice presidency: 99% White
- Senate: 89% White

- House of Representatives: 87% White
- Governors: 98% White
- Mayors: 88% White
- Military advisors: 99% White
- Federal judges: 88% White
- Police officers: 80% White
- People who decide which TV shows we see: 93% White
- People who decide which books we read: 90% White
- People who decide which news is covered: 85% White
- People who decide which music is produced: 95% White
- Schoolteachers: 82% White
- Full-time college professors: 84% White
- Owners of men's pro football teams: 97% White
- Owners of men's pro basketball teams: 98% White[16]

1. Discuss the "Top Decision Makers" chart and list. What are the possible implications of these ratios?
2. Analyze this quote by Thomas Jefferson: "I advance it therefore as a suspicion only, that the blacks, whether originally a distinct race or made distinct by time and circumstances, are inferior to the whites in the endowments both of body and mind." What does it mean?[17]

Activity

The comedian Aamer Rahman discusses reverse racism in a three-minute video called "Fear of a Brown Planet" (posted on YouTube on November 28, 2013). Watch the video and discuss whether Rahman's interpretation matches what we've said in this chapter about the subject.

Chapter 3

"NON-RACIST" IS NOT A THING

> When I was growing up, everyone I knew said they were colorblind. People in my predominantly White community seemed to think that if we ignored race, then racism would go away. We thought this was actually the good and respectful way to be. We thought colorblindness could end racism because we thought racism was about refusing to serve Black people at the lunch counter, or standing in the doorways of schools that were being integrated to deny entrance to Black children. We didn't realize that racism was built into our government, our banking systems, the decision makers working to keep our community all White. We thought colorblindness could end racism because we didn't really understand what racism was. —Ali

Colorblind Racism

Where did the idea of colorblindness come from? White people often refer back to Dr. Martin Luther King, Jr.'s "I Have a Dream" speech, in which he talks about his dream

that one day his children might be judged by the content of their character and not the color of their skin. This idea seemed to provide a simple and immediate solution to racial tensions: pretend that we don't see race, and racism will end. In reality, Dr. King spoke about racial justice, economic justice, and an end to militarism. He wasn't interested in not seeing color; he was trying to create just systems that humanized people of all racial and cultural backgrounds. He was invested in *creating* a world in which race didn't matter, which is not the world we currently live in. Reducing his "I Have a Dream" speech to colorblindness actually runs counter to what he asked of us.

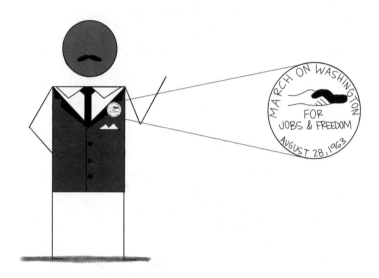

This faulty idea about colorblindness—pretending that race doesn't matter will make it not matter—is still widespread in US society today, and it has led to what sociologist Eduardo Bonilla-Silva calls racism without racists.[1] We have reached a point in US history where racism is so woven into the fabric of our society that we don't actually need people to try to be racist in order for racism to continue. As long as White people ignore race and racism, the fabric of our society remains unchanged. While we may want to be colorblind because we don't want race to matter, colorblindness has the ironic impact of making race matter more. Colorblindness ignores the ways in which race does matter in society, and it helps the racism in our institutions become normalized and

EDUARDO BONILLA-SILVA

YOU CANNOT GO BACK AND PRETEND YOU DON'T KNOW THE TRUTH. YOU HAVE TO DEAL WITH THE GOOD AND THE BAD. YOU CAN'T GO BACK.

Dr. Eduardo Bonilla-Silva is a Black Puerto Rican Distinguished Professor of Sociology at Duke University. Some of his most notable research is about race theory, racial grammar, Whiteness, and colorblind racism. His book *Racism Without Racists: Color-Blind Racism and the Persistence of Racial Inequality in America* helps explain the ways that racism looks in today's society. And according to Dr. Bonilla-Silva, when we know more about how racism works today, we can no longer ignore its effects.[2]

accepted. For this reason, Bonilla-Silva calls colorblindness "colorblind racism" because it allows racism to persist.

Remember the moving walkway? The reason we can have racism without racists is because the walkway was already moving long before we were born. When we take a "colorblind" or "non-racist" stance, we simply ride the moving walkway, which allows us to benefit from and participate in a racist system without any conscious effort. This is why there is no non-racism. The only way to begin to address and change racism is to move the other way on the moving walkway.[3] That is anti-racism, which is active.

CIVIL AND VOTING RIGHTS

"The Civil Rights Act of 1964 prohibits discrimination on the basis of race, color, religion, sex, or national origin.... The act prohibited discrimination in public accommodations and federally funded programs. It also strengthened the enforcement of voting rights and the desegregation of schools.... Passage of the act ended the application of Jim Crow laws."[4] The Civil Rights Act, which declared discrimination unconstitutional, is widely considered to be a piece of landmark legislation. The Voting Rights Act of 1965 began to challenge the barriers to Black voting in the South.[5] As an example of how we have to continue to pay attention, in 2013 key parts of the Voting Rights Act were overturned and many of those protections are now gone.

Racial Talk Versus Racist Talk

How do we talk about race if we've been told that to talk about race is racist? A useful distinction that comes from anthropologists Michael Omi and Howard Winant involves paying attention to the difference between racial talk and racist talk.[6]

Reflect: What do you think the difference is?

Racial talk is talk about race that is supposed to help us understand it better. Racial talk is about how race impacts our lives, how race is part of who we are, part of our experiences and communities. Racial talk helps us confront racism.

Racist talk, on the other hand, reinforces racism. It stereotypes and demeans. It perpetuates the racial hierarchy.

I remember passing out bread to campers when I was a camp counselor. As each person approached me, I would offer them a piece of bread, saying, "Brown or White?" "Brown or White?" "Brown or White?" One of them jokingly said, "Ali, you're being racist! You're making us choose between Brown and White!" I was mortified, in spite of the fact that what I was saying wasn't racist talk. It wasn't even racial talk! It was about food, not race. But still, even the joking suggestion of racism was enough to make me question myself. The distinction between racial talk and racist talk helps me get over my fear that any talk about race or color is racist. Without this distinction, I couldn't talk about race. If I couldn't talk about race, there's not much I could do about racism. —Ali

In the past few years, historian Ibram X. Kendi has given a name to a subcategory of racial talk: anti-racist talk. Kendi would say that racist talk blames individuals for group-level disparities. Anti-racist talk, on the other hand, blames policies and systems for group-level disparities—and helps us see how to change them.

As an example, take this fact: in most major American cities, White people have ten times the net financial worth of Black people.[7] How do we explain this difference, which is evident at the group level? The fact that it's a group-level difference means that it is a pattern we can generalize by race. How can a whole group be wealthier than another whole group? Racist talk would blame individuals: Black people are lazy, they don't care about education, they don't work hard. Notice how these explanations draw on common false stereotypes as well. The story goes that their individual faults explain why they have one-tenth the net financial worth of White people.

But here's the thing, racist explanations don't hold water because they don't account for the actual laws and policies that prevented Black people *as a group* from moving ahead at the same pace as White people *as a group*. Beyond that, we know that race is a social construction and that intelligence and capacity for hard work are evenly distributed among racial groups.[8] Hmmmm. So what could explain the difference? Kendi says that anti-racist ideas blame policies. When we look to the policies that have impacted Black people, they include policies that kept Black people from buying houses in the suburbs, from qualifying for mortgages, from accessing government programs for home building and education, from joining unions, from working professional-wage jobs, from accessing college, etc. There are countless policies we could point to that explain the racial disparities in wealth accumulation. These explanations are more credible because they point to actual historical proof of inequitable treatment of a whole group, rather than stereotypical misperceptions of the individual actions of members of that group.

Aversive Racism

Psychologists at Yale have developed a strand of research that attempts to demonstrate the impact of "non-racism" on groups. The research team divided White participants into three types based on an assessment: "racist," "anti-racist," and "aversive racists."[9]

The people who were identified as "racist" were people who held overt (obvious and conscious) prejudice. The people who were identified as "anti-racist" had very little overt prejudice as well as very little unconscious prejudice. The people who were identified as "aversive racists" did not

> **Implicit bias** is also referred to as unconscious bias. It happens when people make assumptions about another person based on their unconscious beliefs about that person's group identity. These are assumptions about social groups (race, class, gender, ability, etc.) that we have absorbed from the culture around us and are not consciously aware that we have.
>
> DEFINITION

have overt, conscious prejudice, but they scored high on measures of unconscious racial prejudice. In other words, the "aversive racists" believed that racism is wrong, but they had not taken action to address their own *implicit bias*.

The researchers wanted to know what would happen if an "aversive racist" White person was paired with a Person of Color to do a project.[10] Would that team be more or less effective at completing their task than the team composed of an "overtly racist" White person and a Person of Color? Or would the team made up of an "anti-racist" White person and a Person of Color prove to be most effective?

The researchers paired members of each of the types of White people with People of Color to perform a task. The teams that included an "anti-racist" White person and a Person of Color were the fastest and most effective of the three. Which do you think the second-fastest and second-most-effective pairing was?

The surprising finding was that the second-fastest and second-most-effective pairing was the pairing of a Person of Color with an "overtly racist" White person. Why do you think this would be the second-fastest and second-most-effective team?

The pairing with the "overtly racist" White person was a pairing in which the Person of Color knew where they stood with their teammate. They could quickly get to the task at hand because they had more clarity about what they could and could not expect from their partner.

The teams containing a person identified as non-racist, or what the researchers referred to as "aversive racist," were the slowest and least effective. The researchers surmised that this was because the "aversive racists" often acted from unconscious bias, but didn't realize they did so. They did not want to be racist, but they did not feel comfortable working with a Partner of Color. They sent mixed messages that hindered clear communication with their partners.

Researchers projected that same-race pairing would yield even faster and more effective teams than any of the interracial teams, because intergroup racism would essentially be removed from the equation. This suggestion means that in predominantly White institutions, including schools, People of Color are almost always placed on teams that are likely suboptimal for them. Think about it: the majority of White people tend to qualify as "aversive racists," or non-racists. They believe they have no racism, but in fact they have unacknowledged implicit bias. And People of Color rarely get to work with other People of Color in most mainstream organizations; they are regularly paired with White people on teams. This means that People of Color are most often placed in work teams that will likely be the least effective teams they could be a part of—not because of their own skill or lack thereof, but because of the lack of awareness of racism and implicit bias of the White partners on the teams. Meanwhile, if White people are in the majority, they are statistically likely to be randomly paired with other White people most of the time, which is the most effective possible pairing for them.

As this study shows, our implicit biases—and our lack of conscious awareness of those biases—lead to aversive racism. This type of racism is subtle and hard for White people to acknowledge because it is hard to reconcile a conscious desire to not be racist with an unconscious tendency to have racial bias. But this is precisely why there is no such thing as non-racism. Non-racism might as well be called "head-in-the-sand" racism or "fingers-in-my-ears-while-singing-loudly" racism. It's a stance that ignores the reality of racism—both the racism in the world and the bias it creates inside us—so that individuals can feel good about themselves. The inclination is absolutely understandable, because this same study also showed that very few White people *actively want* racism to have such an outsized role in our society or in their relationships. But in order to make that so, we need White people to recognize racism and intervene in it, rather than ignore it. The only way past is through.

Who Benefits from Not Seeing Race?

As you can see from the studies on aversive racism, White people are barely impacted by aversive racism in terms of their productivity. White people can completely ignore race and racism and still be paired most frequently with other White people in fast and highly effective teams. They may be less effective on the rare occasions that they are paired with People of Color, but even then the prevailing wisdom in the racial caste system would suggest that those rare instances are actually the fault of the People of Color. After all, White people can point to the evidence of their effectiveness on all-White teams to demonstrate that it's not about them.

Aversive racism or non-racism is easier for White people to practice and, in fact, benefits White people because it holds in place a system that suggests they are superior to People of Color. For decades, White people have traded a false belief in an equitable society for the option to see themselves as non-racist. But in reality, the idea of non-racism does not get us any closer to an equitable society than holding oneself back from throwing garbage out the window would get us closer to fixing climate change. It's good to not actively litter, but there's much more to do to impact the institutions and systems that damage the Earth.

Aversive racism makes it hard to establish a shared reality. If Students of Color face racism, but their White counter-parts cannot see what they are experiencing, it's as if they live in two different worlds. To build authentic relation-ships and create shared experiences between the two groups, either Students of Color will have to deny their own reality and pretend to be colorblind (which is not only difficult; it's potentially dangerous), or White students will need to acknowledge the reality of racism and their part in it. This can also be difficult, but much less so when you understand two things: (1) you didn't choose your socialization and (2) this acknowledgement allows you to actually interrupt rac-ism. Being in authentic community with one another requires that we build an understanding of a shared reality in which we recognize how we have been divided against each other in a racial caste structure that none of us asked for.

Yeah, but... **it's hard to focus on all this race stuff when climate change is such an imminent threat.**

It's hard to focus on *anything* when we remember the urgency of climate change! That's true. But people who study climate change are becoming increasingly certain that climate justice cannot happen without racial justice. And racial justice cannot happen without climate justice. Why not?

People of Color are disproportionately impacted by climate change. In the US, White people actually breathe cleaner air while also being responsible for more of the consumption patterns that pollute the air.[11] Because of historical housing patterns, low-income communities and Communities of Color are more likely to be located next to airports, highways, train tracks, factories, bus depots, and other sources of pollution. This fact also accounts for higher than average rates of asthma in Black communities.[12]

Globally speaking, we know that the countries most impacted by rising sea levels are nations populated by People of Color. As David Lammy, a Black member of the UK Parliament, says, "The exploitation of natural resources has always been tied to the exploitation of People of Color. Climate change is 'colonialism's natural conclusion.'"[13]

This is what it looks like globally, but how does racism hold back the climate movement at the individual and group levels? One way is that the leading climate-action organizations are led predominantly by White people. We're not saying that those organizations shouldn't exist, but we can't truly address climate change globally without Leaders of Color from around the world being involved in this work. Not because of a superficial need to look "diverse," but because climate change is a worldwide problem that literally cannot be addressed without the input and experience of the people who are most impacted. That means they can't just be offered seats at the table; they need to be at the forefront of our thinking about climate.

It's also a problem related to individual-level prejudice. The local chapter of a robust climate-activism organization in our neighborhood just lost two young, thoughtful Activists of Color because the predominantly White volunteer members of the youth-led organization repeatedly disregarded their voices. This story echoes the story of Vanessa Nakate, a twenty-four-year-old Ugandan activist who posed for a picture with fellow climate activists from around the globe at the Davos World Economic Forum in 2020. When the AP published the photo, only her four White peers were in it; she had been cropped out! As Vanessa said about the photo, "You didn't just erase a photo. You erased a continent."[14] Prompted by that incident, she wrote the book *A Bigger Picture: My Fight to Bring a New African Voice to the Climate Crisis*. Think about how easy it was for that photographer or photo editor to exclude African involvement in climate action by cutting out one person. Their action perpetuates the image that the climate movement is by White people for White people. Seeing Vanessa's face in media across the globe is part of showing that this is not and does not have to be the case. And global struggles to prevent climate change cannot be successful if people from the African continent are not a part of them.

So what do we do about these issues? The skills that readers of this book can gain in terms of the capacity to recognize and intervene in racism will enable you to take action for the climate in ways that are inclusive, multiracial, and mindful of both history and the future.

What Does Non-Racism Look Like in the Real World?

You know non-racism or aversive racism because you've seen it. It looks like colorblindness, yes. But it also looks like the normalization of racial inequality. It looks like statements that equate goodness with Whiteness and badness with Blackness, or foreignness with Asianness and second-class citizenship with Latinx identity.

When people talk about "good schools" and "bad schools" or "good neighborhoods" and "bad neighborhoods," their categorizations often overlap with the racial background of the majority of the residents. "Good schools and neighborhoods" are predominantly White. "Bad schools and neighborhoods" are predominantly Black and Latinx. When we use these explanations to rationalize our choices to participate in racial segregation, that is a form of aversive racism.

Similarly, have you noticed how people will sometimes describe predominantly Black, Latinx, and immigrant neighborhoods as "urban," "diverse," "ghetto," or "sketchy"? These are all terms that are racialized in our collective unconscious but that hide the direct meaning of what we are trying to say when we use them. What are other similarly coded terms? "Single mom," "at-risk youth," "welfare family," "nice young couple."

Explanations rooted in aversive racism are what we come up with when we don't understand the racial inequality all around us. For example, we may ask, "Why is this school or organization predominantly White?" If we don't know the history of racism then it's hard to explain a situation that is the direct result of systemic racism. We end up blaming individuals by expressing ideas such as, "Maybe People of Color aren't interested in attending this school or working here," or "Perhaps People of Color just aren't qualified." When we explain group-level inequality by blaming the individual, we are engaging in the racist talk Kendi describes. Sometimes those explanations are true about particular individuals. But they ignore the racial context of a given Person of Color's perceived "interest" or "qualifications." Usually if a school or organization is predominantly White, that can be explained by looking at its history, who was admitted or permitted to work there, the racial demographics and history of the surrounding community, where the school or organization gets its funding, and the (often unconscious) norms and expectations within the community. This all has a significant impact on performance and outcomes.

Here are some more examples of how aversive racism gets expressed:

- denying that we have limited cross-racial relationships by focusing on a few superficial interactions
- attributing inequality between White people and People of Color to causes other than racism
- assuming the honors and gifted classes are predominantly White because White people are smarter or care more about education

What Does Non-Racism Sound Like in the Real World?

I attended a highly selective college that was located in a majority Black town. When I first arrived on campus, we were told, "You are on an island in

shark-infested waters." The shark-infested waters
they were referring to was the Black community
that surrounded the campus. The average SAT score
for the college was 1400 out of 1600. My score was
1090. The average ACT score for the college was 33
out of 36. My score was 23. When my roommate
asked me what my scores were, I was honest. Her
next question was "How did you get in?" She didn't
need to say, "You got in because you were Black."
But I felt it and second-guessed myself for the rest of
my time in school. I held this feeling of inferiority as
a Black person, and I still fight it today. No one had
to say, "You aren't smart," or "People who look like
you are dangerous." It was implied. —Toni

Yeah, but... **if your scores were lower than the average, maybe that wasn't the right school for you. Maybe
you'd be happier at a school where you were more qualified. Maybe you were taking the place of someone who
was more qualified.**

Whether a student is *qualified* to get into a particular college is based on a number of factors. Scores on standardized
tests are one of many different qualifications that colleges
look at when admitting students, such as grades, letters of
recommendation, activities, athletics, leadership, and potential. Studies have shown that scores on standardized tests are
not predictive of success in college or beyond.[15] The students
who score the highest on standardized tests often have access
to test-prep courses or tutoring. Test scores are highly corre-
lated with income. A student from a low-income background
may have lower test scores, but have a steeper arc to their
growth curve based on their motivation and self-reliance.

Incidentally, it is also somewhat common for a student to get into college because of a parent or grandparent who attended that college (often called legacy admissions). White students and upper-middle-class students benefit overwhelmingly from such policies. Often these legacy admissions waive test scores.

Toni's story from her early years in college demonstrates what Toni Morrison's term "race talk" looks like. Race talk is different from both racial talk and racist talk. Race talk is when we are talking about race without saying "race." Race talk is "the explicit insertion into everyday life of racial signs and symbols that have no meaning other than positioning African Americans into the lowest level of the racial hierarchy."[16] Race talk is racist talk in camo. A common example is the way people on the news express shock that a crime was committed in a White neighborhood. They often say, "We never expected something like that would happen here." This begs the question "Where did you expect it would happen?"

It's impossible to *not see* race in a society organized by race. But attempting to pretend that we can't see race means that we cannot see racism. This is important because although racism is built into our systems, it also lives in us. Toni learned that she would face assumptions that she was inferior. She got this message from living in a society structured by the racial hierarchy. But it's not only People of Color who get such messages. White people also learn their places from living in the racial hierarchy, and what they often learn is a sense of superiority or belonging. That may have been part of what was going on for Toni's roommate as she questioned Toni's SAT scores as well as her presence at an elite college. When a White person is actively anti-racist, they open themselves up to the possibility that they might have internalized superiority or racial bias. They lean toward seeing that bias and understanding it so they do not act on it in unconscious ways. When people point out such bias or racism, an anti-racist White person responds by taking in the feedback and using it to do better, rather than resisting or defending themselves against it. We cannot change what we refuse to see. Anti-racism is about recognizing and intervening with racism both outside and in. In the endnotes for this chapter, you will find an update to Toni's story.[17]

It may feel counterintuitive that being anti-racist means becoming comfortable with the fact that one might have racism inside them and being willing to look for it or receive feedback on it. But consider this: white fragility is the opposite. White fragility comes from trying to be non-racist and feeling like one has to protect oneself against any allegation of racism in order to maintain and protect one's self-image.

We can't change what we refuse to see.

—Robin

Backstage Racism

For anyone who wants to contribute to the dismantling of the racial hierarchy, it's important to know how we (often unwittingly) participate in it. One of the ways this happens for White people is through "frontstage" and "backstage" racism. These are the terms that researchers Leslie Picca and Joe Feagin apply to racism that happens in front of People of Color (frontstage) and racism that happens in all-White groups (backstage).[18] White people frequently find themselves in backstage situations where there are no People of Color to witness or stop them from expressing racism. The researchers asked 626 White college students at twenty-eight colleges across the US to keep journals and record every instance of racial issues, racial images, and racial understanding that they observed or were a part of for six to eight weeks.

Consider this example from their study, related by a young White woman named Ashley: "Robby was there telling a joke. . . . He glanced to see if anyone was around. He starts, 'A black man, a Latin man, and a white guy find a magical lamp on the beach. (Racist joke ensues.)' I thought it was pretty funny and I wasn't the only one. But, I'm glad he waited till no one was around to tell it. If you didn't know Robby you might misunderstand."

If you were in this situation, what would you have done?

A. Laughed
B. Told another racist joke
C. Ignored Robby
D. Stayed silent
E. Changed the subject
F. Told Robby the joke is racist
G. Said, "I don't think that's funny"
H. Talked about how racist it was when Robby wasn't around
I. Left
J. Other

The researchers gathered thousands of examples like this one, and they observed three common themes:

1. Young White people are exposed to and participate in explicit backstage racism with much more frequency than was formerly thought.
2. Many young White people believe that if someone is a good person, they can't be racist.
3. Young White people often excuse and deny even obvious racism by insisting that the perpetrator is a good person, so what they said could not have been racism.

Ashley said that she was glad no one was around to "mis-understand" the joke because, presumably, she believed that Robby didn't mean to be racist; he was just telling a joke. But jokes like these reinforce the racial hierarchy that says People of Color are laughable, that their lives and experiences are not as valuable as those of White people. And even though such jokes do not immediately hurt People of Color since they do not hear the joke, they hurt both People of Color and White people by reinforcing that they are unequal and should be separate.

Sometimes White people feel it's not their place to say something about a racist joke because the joke doesn't directly target them. But White people can be offended by racism too. If racist jokes reinforce a racial hierarchy that you are not interested in holding up, you can be offended no matter your racial background. Any White person who found themselves in that backstage scenario could say, "Hey, that's offensive," or "I don't think making fun of Black people is funny." Or even just shake their head and say something like, "Not funny."

In this particular scenario, one person told the joke. But that was not the only role that White people played in perpetuating the dynamics observed by these research-ers. Backstage conversations like this one typically included people playing the following roles:

Protagonist:	instigator of racist joke/action/behavior
Cheerleader:	colludes through laughter or affirmation
Spectators:	those that stand by passively
Dissenter:	objects to the racist joke/action/behavior

Dissenters appeared much less frequently in the scenarios told by students like Ashley. And when they did speak, what do you think they were told?

"Lighten up."

"It's just a joke."

"So we can't even tell jokes anymore?"

This example demonstrates how racism is all around us. As we discussed in Chapter 1, racism is a system. But it is reinforced by our participation in it. It gets interrupted when we refuse to participate, when we challenge and dissent.

This doesn't mean that you have to cut the Robbys of the world out of your life forever and shun them. Everybody can learn. But we have to get away from this idea that if you are a "good person" you can't be racist. People who grow up in a racial hierarchy (including all people in the US) are going to have some internalized racism that they need to challenge. Robby said something offensive in that example, but it could have easily been any other person. We have all internalized aspects of this system, and we need to help each other unlearn it. Yes, you might get dismissed and told to "lighten up," but you would be in your integrity as someone who claims to be against racism. Unless White people start speaking up and making it uncomfortable to tell racist jokes, they are still getting moved by the walkway. Robby can't get away with his racist jokes without having an audience, so those who are silent are just as complicit with racism as he is.

In my house I learned that some jokes were off limits. But I didn't see what it looked like to stand up to people who were telling racist jokes. If anything, someone would mention after the joke teller left, "That's not an appropriate joke." But I didn't see what it looked like to say that to a person's face. I didn't see how you could intervene with someone, hold them to a higher standard, and still stay in connection. —Ali

Yeah, but... **why would you want to stay in connection with a racist?**

We choose not to call people "racists" but to describe the action as racist. So we'd rephrase the question as "Why would you want to stay in connection with a person who tells racist jokes?" There are lots of reasons that people stay in connection with other people who are imperfect: maybe you are going to keep seeing them anyway because they live across the street and you carpool together; maybe she is your aunt and you will see her every Thanksgiving no matter how much you hate what she says; maybe you sit at the same lunch table and have friends in common. . . . It's hard to just cut people out of your life. So while that's certainly an option, if it's the only option people have, lots of people will just resort to doing nothing. They end up being silent and talking about others behind their backs.

Remember the story of Derek Black from chapter 2 and the impact his friends had on him by not cutting him off but not remaining silent either? We recommend speaking up against the joke rather than simply cutting off all contact with that person. And when you do, remember that everyone is capable of learning, but also be prepared to be met with white fragility.

Robby needs people around him to say, "Hey—that's not funny," and then to help him keep learning. Speaking up will likely be uncomfortable in the moment, but we can't challenge racism and also be comfortable. In fact, White people's comfort around the status quo of racism keeps the walkway moving. The beauty of being exposed to backstage racism is that White people have the unique opportunity to recognize and intervene with racism that is often hidden around People of Color. It's a chance to talk about and challenge the racial hierarchy openly and honestly. And if White people won't do that with each other, who will?

One of the main factors that makes it hard for White people to talk about racism is that the mainstream, popularly-agreed-upon definition of "racism" is simplistic. In the next chapter, we will go into more detail about why racism is more than intentionally hurtful language or acts of violence. That, too, is racism, to be sure, but unfortunately it's just the tip of a much bigger, much more dangerous iceberg.

Afterthoughts

ACTIVITY

Using role-play with a group of people, practice ways to be a dissenter during a backstage conversation. Here are a few scenarios to choose from:

- A friend uses a derogatory term to describe a Person of Color (during the role-play, do not use the actual word).
- You see a racist meme on a friend's social media.
- Someone in your friend group makes a stereotypical comment about a group of People of Color.
- Use *your own* real-world examples. (It is important that you use a personal example, not an example from someone else who is not a part of your group.)

DISCUSSION

In the original book, Robin writes that she does not believe that younger people are less racist than older people. Without stating whether you agree with her or not, draw from everything you've read so far to answer the following question: Why would someone who studies racism say this?

Chapter 4

HOW DOES RACE SHAPE THE LIVES OF WHITE PEOPLE?

We hope it's clear by now that racism is a system that thrives when the people operating within it don't see it, can't talk about it, and consider it normal. The system also thrives when we are divided against one another. In fact, the original design of racism was to make White people and Black people believe they do not, could not, should not, and would not ever have common cause. So when we unite in opposition to this system, our very unity undermines the design of racism. There are two very important points for White people to remember as we talk about the system of racism:

1. You did not create this system. You did not ask for it. This means that although you are well positioned to do something about it, you do not have to feel guilty about it. Nor should you feel guilty about confronting it.
2. If you are a White person who grew up within this system, you are probably going to demonstrate some of the patterns of white fragility—that is part of how the system keeps going. Recognizing those patterns can help White people do the rewiring that makes them better equipped to confront racism.

As Oluo says in the quote below,[1] the system itself thrives on the ignorance of White people, on the ongoing

Ijeoma Oluo is a Nigerian American writer and public speaker. Her book *So You Want to Talk About Race* was a *New York Times* best seller in 2018. Oluo describes herself as an "Internet Yeller." She began her writing career as a blogger after the death of Trayvon Martin, and she has continued to use her writing to promote ongoing conversations about racial dynamics. Her most recent book, *Mediocre*, is about how dangerous it is for everyone when White men have social power that is granted based on their race and gender rather than their skills and qualifications.

disconnection between White people and People of Color, on the segregation of our lifestyles and the separation of our realities.

In this chapter, we're going to talk about how race shapes the lives of White people. This can be hard for White people to see—kind of like looking at the color red through rose-colored glasses. But being White has a big impact on White people's lives. So how *does* race shape the lives of White people? We will give several examples throughout this chapter, including:

- how White people are seen as "just people"
- the belonging and freedom that come with being White
- racial separation in housing that makes segregation seem "natural"
- White racial innocence
- the pressure to maintain White solidarity

As you'll see by the end of the chapter, each of these aspects of the impact of race on White people is a contributing factor to white fragility.

Just People

As we laid out in Chapter 1, Whiteness translates into a "norm" in that it becomes the reference point. We see it everywhere, but we don't talk about it. For example, in fiction, characters are described by hair color and sometimes body type, but their race is usually named only if they are not White. In the news, People of Color are described racially, while the Whiteness of White people is left unsaid. In schools, if an author is a Person of Color, the teacher might talk about that. But if they are White, their Whiteness usually remains unspoken. Maya Angelou was a Black writer, for example, while Jane Austen was just a writer.

Most of "the classics" or works in "the canon" are widely respected because they are seen as a foundational base for an educated person. The ideal "educated person" in this scenario is a White person, rooted in knowledge of Western Europe, familiar with Greek myths, knowledgeable about European and American writers. Although today schools throughout the country have begun to understand the importance of teaching beyond "the canon," there is still a tendency to add to the curriculum without taking anything away. Work that familiarizes students with ancient African kingdoms, Aztec mythology, or Chinese literature is too often seen as additional or optional. These are histories and literatures that are critical to helping People of Color see the value of their own ancestry while helping White students appreciate the rich history and contributions of many different traditions. In a healthy, racially integrated society, everyone would get to learn about their own history, and their classmates would learn it too.

Educators call this type of expansive curriculum "windows and mirrors."[2] Every person needs to encounter mirrors of themselves in the books they read, the history they learn, and the role models and images they see around them. White students in the US tend to have plenty of mirrors, while most Students of Color have very few, if any. Students also need windows into the lives of people who are different from them—racially and otherwise. Most Students of Color have plenty of windows into the lives of White people. But White people have few windows into the lives, experiences, and perspectives of People of Color. When educators create mirrors for Students of Color, White students get windows. This is part of how White people begin to counter unconscious superiority: remembering that one's White worldview is not universal. When anyone's worldview is expanded, everybody wins.

Anthropologist Ruth Frankenberg created one of the most widely used definitions of Whiteness. As you will see, it's not just about *being White*. It's about the meaning that Whiteness began to have when White people were put at the top of the racial hierarchy. Frankenberg helps explain how Whiteness can be both invisible and incredibly impactful. Here is how she describes it: "First, whiteness is a location of structural advantage, of race privilege. Second, it is a 'standpoint,' a place from which white people look at ourselves, at others, and at society. Third, 'whiteness' refers to a set of cultural practices that are usually unmarked and unnamed."[3]

Notice that *Whiteness* is not about having light, pinkish skin or even having European ancestry. It's not about phenotypically (in terms of skin color) being White. Whiteness is about (1) where White people are placed on a false hierarchy, (2) the lens through which White people see themselves and others, and (3) White ways of doing things that are often taken for granted as normal and therefore better.

When the generic or anonymous representation of "human" is depicted, it is usually based on the assumption that people are White. When Toni and Ali were little, Crayola had a peach-colored crayon called "Flesh." This is an example of Whiteness at work in the world: the skin tone of many White people was considered to be the definition of the color labeled "flesh." While that is no longer the case with crayons, the tendency to use Whiteness as the norm continues to show up in the following practices and products:

- depictions of Jesus, God, angels, and other religious figures
- make-up foundation that presumes pinkish skin
- adhesive bandages
- dummies for CPR training
- mannequins

- the majority of dolls
- educational models of the human body
- Legos

> *I can remember taking my kids to Fairy Friday at
> the Botanical Gardens and seeing all the posters
> and flags of fairies depicting pale-skinned, winged
> fairies. I thought, "If they have wings, then they are
> definitely not real. Why, then, can't we depict them
> with different skin colors?" —Ali*

Seeing yourself in the world around you may seem
superficial, but it validates and affirms a person's existence.
Displaying representations of only one racial group suggests
that it is the only racial group that matters. It suggests that
only White children deserve to imagine themselves as part of
a fantasy, or only White people belong at that event. Perhaps
more starkly, it suggests that the people running the venue,
making the Band-Aids, and designing the posters simply
don't think of People of Color as part of their world. Or that
perhaps the lives of People of Color don't matter.

> *My dad owned a small business. It was not lost on
> him that anytime a customer had an issue with him
> they would ask to see the manager. They would
> assume that he, a Black man, couldn't be the man-
> ager. He described loving their sense of surprise
> when he would answer them with, "I am not the
> manager, but I am the owner." —Toni*

Belonging and Freedom

I have always experienced racial belonging as a White person. This was hard for me to see at first because it was just so normal. I sometimes felt excluded in certain conversations because of my curly hair or my lack of belonging in a clique at school, but I never felt like I experienced reality in a completely different way from the people around me. The first time I really experienced what it feels like to not belong racially was in college when I went to an anti-racism event coordinated by a multiracial classmate of mine, who was Black and Chinese American. It was the first time I was in the minority racially. I can remember feeling relieved that I had been formally invited because I needed reassurance that I belonged there. My classmate who invited me became a lifeline for me because I knew no one else in the room. My own awareness of my Whiteness—my difference from most of the group—was heightened. I became less sure of what I should say or how I should interact. I felt tense and insecure. It was the opposite of how I felt in most public meetings at my college, where I was usually in the racial majority without even realizing it. —Ali

The racial belonging that comes from being White feels normal and unconscious to White people who see it all around them most of the time. White people see themselves in magazines, TV shows, "most beautiful" lists, makeup, teachers, therapists, classmates, history, heroes and heroines, textbooks, lifeguards, camp counselors, dentists, doctors, principals—the list goes on. Students of Color often share that they have been told they are "Pretty for an Asian girl" or "On the list of most beautiful Black girls." Let's be clear that assessing anyone's beauty—especially in ranked-list form— can only end in hurt and exclusion. But when people make separate lists for different racial groups, it's one more way in which Whiteness is established as the measure of beauty, while People of Color are seen as beautiful only within their own category—not comparable to the White standard. The most beautiful people on the White list are not explicitly identified as White. Their Whiteness is normalized by being unnamed.

The term "**racialized**," like the term "**minoritized**," is meant to convey that the status of race or of being a minority is attributed to People of Color from the outside. As we have learned, White people don't tend to experience racialization—it's much more common for White people to be seen as individuals before they are seen as White people.

DEFINITION

The one big challenge to the sense of racial belonging that White people experience is when they find themselves, as Ali did, in a space that is majority People of Color. The sense that they don't belong is rare—and often something they have to seek out themselves. It is not a position that most White people find themselves in unintentionally.

This transfers to other parts of life where being in all-White or predominantly White spaces starts to feel more comfortable and easier than being in mixed spaces. People make choices about where to drive, where to exercise, where to go to school, where to locate their business, where to live, whom to talk to, whom to befriend, even whom to marry based on what feels comfortable. The racial aspect of their choices is usually invisible to them. White people become so used to being racially comfortable that they can become self-conscious and awkward on the rare occasion when they are in the minority. For people who are in the racial minority most of the time, on the other hand, racial comfort is not something they can take for granted.

> *I recently had the brilliant idea that I would "beat the traffic" and drive through the night from Philadelphia to North Carolina to visit my family, a drive I have made at least thirty times during the day. About two hours from where my family lives, I got really sleepy. Pulling over was not an option. Unlike in the early 2000s, when I started making that drive, those miles of Virginia highway are now filled with Trump signs and Confederate flags. There is no 2021 version of The Green Book, a travel guide that Black motorists carried with them when driving in the Jim Crow South from the 1930s to the 1970s. The book gave pointers on where it was safe for Black travelers to stop for the night, where they could use the bathroom, who would sell them gas. I told my copilot that we couldn't stop. We turned up the music and the air conditioning and fought our way through the sleepiness. —Toni*

Racial belonging becomes a form of freedom. It's the freedom to speak up when you have something to say, and the freedom to drive through the night without a second thought whether you're in rural North Carolina, New York City, or the suburbs of Springfield, Illinois.

Yeah, but... **not all White people automatically feel a sense of belonging in US society.**

That's true. White people who have marginalized identities, including those who are gay, trans, or working class, for example, may not feel automatic belonging in US society, or may have to face constant questioning about their lives and identities. But to the extent that White gay, trans, and working-class people see themselves reflected in the society around them, they see a reflection of their Whiteness. In *The Guide for White Women Who Teach Black Boys*, a young Black trans man wrote about seeing White trans men as well as Black cis men as role models.[4] But when he looked around, he couldn't see any visible Black trans men whom he could look to for support or inspiration. While all young trans people need more out trans role models and out trans allies to be visible to them,[5] White trans people have many more mirrors in popular society than do trans People of Color. And trans People of Color often experience racism in the wider trans community. This is why windows and mirrors matter so much for people from marginalized groups. They acknowledge and affirm a person's existence and reality. They affirm that you belong.

Time Travel: A Viable Option for People of Color?

Remember the slogan "Make America Great Again"? It attempted to appeal to people who believe that the US's best days are behind us, that some kind of societal goodness

existed just fifty years ago—a goodness we could and should return to. But the view that there was such a thing as "the good old days" is rooted in a White worldview. Just look at any place in the history of the country and you will find examples of racism. For most People of Color, the good old days were not good. Any time travel to an era before now would take people to a country in which their prospects, opportunities, safety, access to resources, and life circumstances were more restricted than they are today. But this mantra of returning to a past greatness appealed to many White voters who see the past, with its unquestioned racial hierarchy, as beneficial to them. The slogan worked in concert with racist language blaming undocumented workers, immigrants, and the Chinese for problems in the US, shifting the focus away from the people who have the most power in today's society: the White upper-class elite. The romanticized past is not so romantic for everyone.

Here is a brief list of some of the most egregious historical events and eras that demonstrate why time travel to the past would be ill-advised for People of Color:

- 246 years of enslavement
- genocide of Indigenous people
- theft of Indigenous lands and forced relocation
- lynching
- sharecropping
- Chinese exclusion laws
- Japanese American internment
- Jim Crow laws, including bans on Black people testifying against White people
- medical experimentation
- redlining

Segregated Lives

The US is a highly segregated society. Even when explicit Jim Crow–era laws requiring racial segregation were abolished, neighborhoods and cities stayed racially segregated. The segregation was enforced in many different ways, including

THE CHINESE EXCLUSION ACT

The Chinese Exclusion Act of 1882 was the first significant law that restricted immigration into the US. President Chester A. Arthur signed it into legislation after residents of the West Coast blamed the immigration of people from China as the reason for continued low wages—even though the population makeup of the West Coast at the time had less than 1 percent Chinese people. The act, which intended to prevent any immigration from Chinese laborers, was seen as a way of maintaining "racial purity" in the United States.[6]

REDLINING

Redlining is a discriminatory practice followed by banks and other lenders that labeled certain neighborhoods as "dangerous" or "risky" for creditworthiness. The federal Home Owners' Loan Corporation, which performed real estate assessments on different areas of cities, literally drew red lines on maps around neighborhoods that were Black or immigrant.[7] The maps were not only used to determine home values; they also determined who lived in the areas outside the red line. In the 1950s the practice of redlining helped shape the newly growing suburbs as all-White places by restricting banks from giving mortgages to anyone moving out of or into one of the redlined neighborhoods. The effects of those practices are still felt today. People of Color who bought homes within the redlined areas have experienced low home values, which makes it almost impossible to accumulate wealth—unlike in the suburbs, where home values have risen, allowing White people to accumulate and pass down wealth to their children over many decades.[8]

by local governments, through housing policy, through mortgage-lending practices, and even through housing covenants that were written into the deeds of homes, stating that the house could not be sold to a non-White person. A neighborhood's racial makeup becomes the measure of its goodness or badness, safety or danger using the "race talk" we described in the last chapter. It's common to hear people say they grew up in a "nice" neighborhood, referring to a White community. It's common to hear Black and immigrant neighborhoods referred to as "ghetto" or even a "not-so-nice part of town." In 2013, an app was developed called Ghetto Tracker, which was intended to crowdsource "whole geographic areas as 'good' or 'bad,' 'safe' or 'unsafe.'"[9] After being critiqued for its racist and classist undertones, the app was renamed Good Part of Town.

Yeah, but... **isn't it helpful to know what parts of a city are safe or unsafe?**

The problem with technology like this is that it imposes a new form of segregation on cities, in which people from different neighborhoods no longer need to interact with each other. It also assumes that a universal measure of safety exists, which is not true. When Black and Latinx people drive in predominantly White areas, they often get stopped and harassed by police or neighbors. When Ahmaud Arbery was jogging in a White neighborhood, two White men who saw him assumed that he was stealing something. With a friend, they chased him in a pickup truck and shot and killed him. When Trayvon Martin was killed while walking home in his father's gated community of Sanford, Florida, it was because neighbor George Zimmerman thought he looked suspicious, followed him, and shot him. Would the Ghetto Tracker app know where Trayvon Martin—a Black seventeen-year-old— would be safe or unsafe? While many White people might *feel* less safe in a predominantly Black or Latinx community, Black and Latinx people may *be* less safe in a predominantly White community.

Most violent crime in the US is committed by somebody known to the victim. And most violent crime is intraracial, meaning within the same racial group. This is because our country is significantly segregated by race. We've likely heard the term "Black on Black crime," but most violent crime committed against White people is "White on White." Although many White people are socialized to fear Black communities, White people's experiences of violence and trauma most often occur at the hands of other White people, including rape, sexual assault, and abuse. In this way, racism teaches people to be cautious toward the wrong people, thereby making them less safe.

Rates of drug use in White communities are similar to rates of drug use in Black communities, but it is often less visible because White people are more likely to live in single-occupant homes (rather than apartment complexes), therefore having access to private spaces, and having less frequent exposure to a police presence. White people who use drugs are caught less frequently than Black people and experience more lenient sentences when taken to court. Even crack cocaine and powdered cocaine incur different sentences.[10] Possession or dealing of crack, which tends to be associated with Black people, is punished more harshly than possession or dealing of powdered cocaine, even though crack is a form of cocaine.

Schools are affected by this same phenomenon. Often populated by the neighborhoods around them, schools are seen as "good" or "bad" depending on their racial makeup. Many People of Color who have the means to access schools with high test scores are caught in a bind. They may want their children to attend well-resourced schools, but do not want their children to be racially isolated within predominantly White schools or on predominantly White academic tracks. This is not a choice White people have to make. As White people seek out the "best" schools and the highest test scores, they generally end up choosing from among schools and neighborhoods where they are part of the racial majority.

This is how danger, low achievement, and inferiority get associated with Black spaces. Apps like Ghetto Tracker and behaviors that steer White people away from Black and Latinx communities when buying homes and choosing schools reinforce segregation.

In the following quote, renowned Black writer and activist James Baldwin suggests that the question of whether this segregation is intentional is irrelevant. Segregation—and the devaluation of Black and Brown spaces—hurts People of Color.

> I don't know if white Christians hate Negroes or not, but I know that we have a Christian church that is white and a Christian church which is black. I know that the most segregated hour in American life is high noon on Sunday. . . . I don't know whether the labor unions and their bosses really hate me . . . but I know I am not in their unions. I don't know if the real estate lobby is against black people but I know that the real estate lobbyists keep me in the ghetto. I don't know if the Board of Education hates black people, but I know the textbooks they give my children to read and the schools that we have to go to. Now this is the evidence. You want me to make an act of faith risking . . . my life . . . on some idealism which you assure me exists in America which I have never seen.[11]

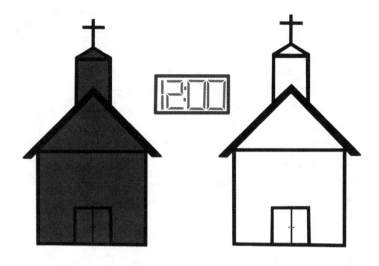

Baldwin spoke those words in the 1960s. Is segregation today as bad as it was during James Baldwin's time? In some ways, it's worse, because segregation occurs at similar rates but we have normalized it as a society.[12] Remember, racism is a highly adaptive system. And while you can see how real estate practices, mortgage-lending policies, or the federal government created segregation, you can also see how individuals maintain it by not questioning or challenging it. Many White people believe that involvement and investment in Black or Latinx communities is dangerous or unprofitable, so people who have the financial means to make those investments choose not to, unless those communities are becoming White. How often have you overheard White people talking about how they purchased a house in an up-and-coming neighborhood and were able to sell that house for many times the original price? What they mean is they bought a house in a neighborhood that was becoming more expensive (often because it was becoming more White), and they profited from that trend. This is how gentrification works.

Middle- and upper-class White people tend to choose segregation when buying homes more often than they choose integration. Working-class White people and poor urban White people are more likely to live in multiracial neighborhoods because poverty puts them in closer proximity to People of Color. But as White people become more upwardly mobile and have more choices in their living conditions, they are more likely to choose Whiter environments that are seen as more desirable. This is not merely a preference to be closer to people more like oneself. Because of the widespread perception that White neighborhoods are better neighborhoods, proximity to Whiteness and White spaces usually translates to greater desirability and, ultimately, more resources.

The racial segregation of our neighborhoods and schools means that White people grow up seeing mostly White people around them. This means that many White people—and even many People of Color—start to take this racialized separation for granted. In the meantime, White people see and experience events in ways that they assume everybody does. When People of Color explain that they have very different views and experiences, they are often not believed. The result is that most White people don't understand how much Whiteness shapes their lives and lenses.

White Racial Innocence

It's a common stereotype that the more People of Color (Black people and Latinx people especially) a neighborhood has, the more dangerous it is. But it is well documented that Black and Latinx folks are stopped by police more often than White folks for the same activities. Most judges are White, and they hand down harsher sentences to People of Color for the same infractions. Criminal behavior in young White people is often seen as "juvenile behavior," while Black youth are often prosecuted as adults. Punishments for the same crimes are much harsher for People of Color than for White people of the same age.[13]

In 2015, a biracial woman named Chanel Miller attended a party at a fraternity at Stanford University. On her way home, she was attacked, dragged behind a dumpster, and raped. She was found by two White cyclists, who restrained her assailant until the police arrived. Had her assailant been Black, there is little doubt that his punishment would have been severe. But Miller's assailant was a White Stanford fraternity member named Brock Turner, known for being a champion swimmer for the college. When Turner went before a White male judge, Aaron Pesky, he faced up to fourteen years in a federal prison. Instead he was sentenced to six months in a county jail. He only served three.[14] Why was the judge so lenient after this heinous crime? The fact that the judge was White—and male—meant that he could relate to the defendant. He believed that six months in a county jail would be enough to help Turner see the error of his ways, and the judge did not want to "ruin his life" over a "mistake" he had made as a young person. Decisions like this—to forgive the so-called mistakes of White youth—happen time and again in schools, with police, and in courts of law, in spite of the fact that Brock Turner was responsible for destroying someone else's life. It wasn't just the judge who saw Turner in a favorable light (rather than as a rapist); one news article actually called him "baby-faced."[15]

Meanwhile, Black youth accused of nonviolent crimes will spend decades in prison for minor—sometimes unproven— offenses.[16] Consider the case of the Exonerated Five (formerly known as the Central Park Five), five Black teenaged boys who each served prison terms of between five and eleven years for a crime they did not commit. Or Kalief Browder, a sixteen-year-old from the Bronx who was accused of stealing a backpack, a crime for which he was never found guilty. Kalief was sent to Rikers Island, a New York City jail, in 2010. He never had a trial. He ultimately spent three years at Rikers, and was held in solitary confinement for two of those years. Two years after he was released, Kalief committed suicide. May his memory be a reminder to all of us why educating ourselves on racism and working to see and change it is so important.

These are two examples among thousands we could offer in which our justice system routinely punishes the wrong people because of racial bias. The assumption of innocence that many give to White people is directly connected to the presumption of guilt for Black people and Latinx people. Delinquent behavior by White juveniles is usually attributed to external factors like home problems or depression— factors that are not the child's fault, thereby voiding their crime. By contrast, the behavior of Juveniles of Color is usually attributed to something internal, like violent psychopathy or criminal intent. In the cases cited above, the lives of completely innocent teenagers were destroyed while a sexual assailant went free with minimal punishment. This is one of the ways that racism hurts everyone—it teaches us to fear and punish people who are not a menace to society while tolerating the behaviors of those who are.

White racial innocence isn't just about being innocent until proven guilty and having the criminal justice system go easy on you. There is another way that the idea of White racial innocence impacts White people—one they don't usually see. It is the expectation that White people don't have to know anything about racism in order to be successful. A White person can become a teacher, a principal, a successful businessperson, a senator, a doctor, a lawyer, a computer engineer, a filmmaker, or nearly any other type of professional without any racial awareness at all, much less any racial skill or commitment to anti-racism, and still be seen as qualified for their jobs. Not only do many White people know very little about racism, but People of Color are often expected to teach White people about race, correct racist behavior, tell them how to not be racist, and generally be the monitors of racism.

This idea comes from the mistaken notion that racism is a problem endured by People of Color that has nothing to do with White people. It comes from the belief that it is the job of People of Color to teach White people about race— regardless of the fact that many resources on race *have* been created by People of Color to educate White people (for a short list, see Additional Resources, at the end of this book). Finally, it neglects to acknowledge how hard it is tell one's story of racism when people aren't ready to hear it. For a Person of Color to teach a White person about their experience of racism, the White person must have enough racial competence to refrain from invalidating the story by saying, "You must be imagining things," or "Maybe that's not what was meant." When a person operates from White racial innocence, they take little personal responsibility for learning and doing something about racism. They rely on People of Color to educate them or monitor them, and often they respond with denial when People of Color do.

White Solidarity

> *I was socialized into White solidarity without knowing it. The people who taught me White solidarity had no idea that was what they were teaching. If a neighbor told a racist joke, I was told not to repeat it . . . but not until that neighbor left. I didn't learn how to speak up in the moment and say, "I don't like jokes that make Black people look foolish." The lesson there was that it was more important to maintain the appearance of unity with my neighbor than to speak up against his racism. —Ali*

White solidarity is probably familiar to you, although you might not have called it that. White solidarity is often unconscious and unspoken. It is literally the silence or laughter that follows a racist joke that people want to confront . . . but don't know how. It is living and working in almost all-White spaces . . . without questioning how those spaces managed to exclude People of Color. It is watching a Friend of Color get teased . . . and not knowing how to support them or speak up. It is hearing other White students mock a Student of Color's name out of earshot . . . and not saying anything. It is avoiding communities and activities that are predominantly made up of People of Color, or spreading rumors that a Person of Color is dangerous, malicious, or suspicious . . . when you would not do the same regarding similar behavior from a White person. It is treating the actions of a White person (such as being asked on a date) as innocent . . . while assuming that when the advance comes from a Person of Color, it is nefarious and suspect. White solidarity, also referred to as collusion, is the unspoken agreement among White people to protect White advantage and to avoid causing another White person to feel discomfort by confronting them when they say or do something racially problematic.

So what happens when White people choose to interrupt White solidarity? What are the consequences?

- Being seen as too sensitive or politically correct
- Feeling like a wet blanket
- Being told you are not a team player
- Gaining the reputation of being judgmental

What are the positive consequences of interrupting White solidarity?

- You realize that your voice matters and has an impact, even when you speak up imperfectly.
- Every time you do it, you gain courage and practice for next time.
- Usually when you speak up, you realize that other people were uncomfortable too.
- You change the tone and expectations of the group.
- People of Color might see you as more trustworthy.
- You get to become a contributing part of a multiracial community, not just a White community.

- You live and act with integrity.
- You're not degraded by humor that brings other people low.

White solidarity is seductive. It can feel bad to break away from the White mainstream and differentiate oneself, especially if the White mainstream is all you have known socially. But White solidarity is a way that racism remains unchecked. It keeps racism and the racial hierarchy in place. Notice how so many of the reasons to maintain White solidarity are about being seen a certain way. They're about wanting to fit in and look cool. The reasons to interrupt White solidarity are about being the person who speaks up, who stands in their integrity, and who is not willing to be degraded or to let others be degraded.

Yeah, but... **I'm conflict avoidant.**

Okay, yes. Being conflict avoidant can make it hard to speak out against the group. Here is some framing that might help with that. If racism is the status quo, the only way to be anti-racist is to go against the status quo. It's hard to do that if you are trying to avoid all conflict. *But*, it is important to distinguish between conflict and fighting. Being anti-racist does not mean you have to start fights everywhere you go. Interrupting White solidarity can take several forms that don't involve a fight. In fact, interrupting White solidarity in a way that helps other White people hear you is often more strategic and effective than doing so in a way that makes them defend themselves and dig in their heels.

As our White readers think about interrupting White solidarity, consider these strategies:

- Relate to the person before disagreeing. Say, "I used to find that funny. But I recently learned that it's actually really offensive. Here's what I've learned . . ."

- Tell the person you have seen their good intention, and let them know that their actions/words are not in sync with that intention. Say, "You seem to really care about people because I see you show up at these events over and over. I thought you'd want to know that the word you're using is actually really hurtful."
- Engage them in inquiry, especially if you don't know why something is a problem. Say, "Ouch, that joke makes me super uncomfortable, but I don't know why." Be open to talking it through with them.
- Sometimes you might be talking to someone who is truly just a bully, and they are not going to hear even the most thoughtful intervention. Remember that when you speak up to them and walk away, you are interrupting White solidarity. Maybe all you can think of is, "That's a crappy thing to say," or, "I don't understand why that's funny." It's okay if you leave them unchanged. Other people will have heard what you said, and it will influence what they do and say in the future. When you interrupt White solidarity—no matter how you do so—you impact the climate of the whole group. Even if that one individual won't change, you make a difference to others by speaking up. And even if no one is there to hear you, you made a difference to yourself.
- If you notice that People of Color—their histories, experiences, and accomplishments—are absent from your curriculum, or you notice a problem with how a group is being portrayed, you can talk to your teacher. This will usually be more effective if you talk with them one on one outside of class, speak from the "I" perspective, and let them know how the curriculum impacts you. Most teachers care about you and want to know how their teaching affects you.

Racial Patterns That Are at the Foundation of White Fragility

Being "woke" isn't enough. When I become aware that the fire alarm is going off in my building, just waking up isn't adequate. I have to do something about it to get myself to safety. —Toni

If you grew up in the US, it's probably hard to imagine what our country would look like if—from the beginning—people of all racial and ethnic backgrounds had been given equal access to opportunities, jobs, labor unions, medical care, education, government protection, legal status, the vote, citizenship, and home ownership. It's even harder to imagine a US where Indigenous relationships to the land were respected and seen as role models for sustainable living, rather than as "barbaric" and "uncivilized" and needing to be eliminated or removed. Racial segregation like we have today is not natural or normal. But many of us have grown up without questioning it and often feel more comfortable within it than in integrated spaces. We don't even realize how much we would benefit from belonging to healthy multiracial communities. We don't see how much White people lose from living and working in all-White spaces. We rarely talk about how racism hurts White people, too—not just by making them complicit in oppression, but in the way that it holds the entire society back.[17]

The most profound message of racial segregation may be that the absence of People of Color in our lives is no real loss.

—Robin

As we wrote at the beginning of the chapter, we want you to remember that you didn't create this system of racism. And if you are growing up in the system as a White person, you likely have experienced the expectation of White racial innocence, or the pull toward White solidarity, without even knowing what it was. We want to emphasize that in a society so heavily organized by racial ideas and constructs, everybody is shaped by them in some way. Understanding white fragility means understanding how growing up in the system teaches White people behaviors and attitudes that preserve racism. Understanding white fragility is the first step in standing up to the system, to wresting back your autonomy, and to saying that you don't want to be a part of it.

Common racial patterns that are foundational to white fragility include:

- Having no understanding of the systemic nature of racism
- Believing that the forces of racial socialization and the messages that surround you don't have any impact on you
- Insisting that everyone is a unique individual, so one's race has no meaning
- Having little knowledge of the history of racism, and how that history impacts the present
- Assuming that People of Color have the same experiences as White people
- Lacking humility
- Believing there's nothing else to know
- Being unwilling to listen and learn further
- Lacking interest in the perspectives and experiences of People of Color
- Wanting to jump past the hard, personal work and rush to solutions; not understanding that self-awareness is the first step

- Valuing not being seen as racist over actually interrupting racism
- Protecting other White people's feelings instead of intervening in racism ("John didn't mean anything, he's a really nice guy")
- Allowing guilt to excuse inaction
- Being too defensive to take in feedback
- Focusing on intentions over impact (insisting, "Since I didn't mean to hurt someone, it shouldn't count that I *did* hurt someone")

At the end of this book, we will offer more ways that you can interrupt racism and the racial hierarchy, not just for yourself but for your friends and classmates. As we said above, interrupting racism doesn't have to mean starting giant conflicts and navigating irresolvable differences. We want to equip you with lots of potential strategies so that both you and your peers and colleagues will be able to shift a culture of racism that hurts everybody.

Afterthoughts

Journal

In this chapter Ali writes about being socialized into White solidarity. The main reason this was her experience is because she grew up in almost all-White spaces. What is your experience of the places where you live and the people that you spend time with? In your journal, write the answers to the following questions, and reflect on the significance of your answers.

- Did your parents tell you that race didn't matter and everyone was equal?
- Is your neighborhood segregated or integrated?
- If you live in a segregated neighborhood, how often do you go into the neighborhoods of people who are a different race than you? For what reasons do you go?
- Have the adults in your life encouraged you to visit the neighborhoods where people of other racial backgrounds live, in order to get to know them? If not, why not? How have they communicated that you shouldn't visit such neighborhoods?
- Who do you sit beside in the cafeteria?
- Are honors classes racially diverse at your school?
- When was the first time you had a teacher of the same race(s) as you? How often has that been the case?
- What is the significance of the answers to these questions?

Chapter 5

THE GOOD/BAD BINARY

In Western culture, we tend to think in terms of binaries: good/bad, right/wrong, guilty/innocent. This is also called either/or thinking.[1] In either/or thinking, either something is good or it is bad—it can't be both. Either/or thinking leaves very little grey area. But it doesn't have to be this way. In many African cultures and Eastern religions, for example, people think in terms of both/and. A person can be both good and bad. An action can have both positive and negative impacts. Human beings and societies are often way too complex for things to be all one thing or the other.

We tend to think of bullying through the perspective of the good/bad binary. Bullies are bad. Victims are good. Experts on bullying say that bullying in schools is actually not that common. But when it does occur, 85 percent of the time it is in front of other students, with no teachers around.[2] Would you call the bystanders good or bad? It's hard to say. They might not even recognize the bullying for what it is. But those same experts say that the students who are bystanders often have the most power to stop the bullying. If bystanders have that power but don't use it, does that make them bad?

Child psychologist Carol Dweck suggests that binaries like these create a fixed mindset.[3] When students say things like "I'm bad at reading" or "I'm a bad athlete," it reinforces the idea that a person can only be good or bad at something— and if they're bad, there's no possible way for them to become good. Dweck suggests turning statements into "not yet" statements by saying, "I'm not good at algebra . . . yet," or "I'm not a fast runner . . . yet." Dweck says we need to have a growth mindset—to see that we can grow our skill sets and become better at things we work at. If I believe I'm a bad writer, then it's hard to ever become better. Instead I could say, "Writing is hard for me today." Or, "I'm not the writer I want to be yet." First we have to believe that our goodness or badness is not permanent; it is not all that we are.

US society tends to think of racism within the either/or framework of the good/bad binary, which tells us that people who are racist are bad and people who are not racist are good. There are several problems with this framework.

First, if doing something racist means you are a bad person, most people will deny they have done something racist, especially if they did not intend to. For example, someone dresses up in Blackface for Halloween, poses in ways that are insulting to Black people, and then posts pictures to Instagram. When people see it and say that it's racist, they deny it because they didn't intend for it to be racist. Or someone suggests that Asian Americans are all good at math. Someone else says that's a racist overgeneralization. The person who made the comment comes back with, "I'm not racist, I have lots of Asian friends." So how do we move forward if we won't consider the possibility that we've hurt someone, even a person we care about, because we think hurting someone means we are a bad person?

Second, if we don't understand racism as a system, then when we hear people saying that White people are at the top of the hierarchy and benefit from racism regardless of their awareness or intentions, we think people are saying that all White people are bad.

Third, it suggests an unmovable binary. Nobody can ever grow, learn, and change if they are just racist or non-racist, good or bad.

Finally, the good/bad binary prevents White people from taking feedback. Instead of learning from the feedback, the person puts their energy into defending their character. It pretty much guarantees defensiveness, and that defensiveness actually ends up protecting racism.

In his hilarious and helpful TEDx talk, Jay Smooth, founder of New York City's longest-running hip hop radio program, WBAI's *Underground Railroad*, said it best when he suggested that we should stop treating racism and prejudice like tonsils, which can be removed.[4] When people operate from the tonsil model, if someone tells them, "I think you might have some unconscious prejudice," they might reply, "That's impossible. I had my racist tonsils removed five years ago." They think in either/or terms: you either have tonsils or you don't. You either have prejudice or you don't.

Jay suggests that racism and prejudice are actually more like plaque that builds up on our teeth. Rather than thinking of oneself as all good or all bad, think instead of being good as "a practice," like brushing your teeth. Good dental hygiene is something that has to be maintained every day. If someone tells me, "Hey, you have some food in your teeth," it wouldn't make sense to say, "What? I brushed my teeth this morning. I couldn't possibly have food in my teeth now." Similarly, if someone says I'm displaying some racism in my thinking, I'm going to take the feedback and work on it. In terms of the good/bad binary, if we continue to think in strict either/or terms, it leaves us no choice but to deny the allegation—to insist our teeth are clean even though they are full of spinach.

After the civil rights movement, many White people across the nation saw "the racists" as Southerners in white KKK hoods who were actively, and violently, trying to reinforce segregation and the second-class status of Black people. Because they themselves didn't practice overt violence or use hateful language, many White people were able to see racists as bad and themselves as good. The problem with this mindset is that it continues to frame racism as individual acts of violence rather than a system. If the racists are always somebody else, then White people can't see how they benefit from a racist system or how they could do something to stop it. In this case, most of the White people in the country were not members of the Klan. But they continued to benefit from a system in which they received preferential treatment for education, jobs, union membership, home ownership, medical care, participation in community clubs, and so on. In fact, groups like the Klan depended on the silence of those "not

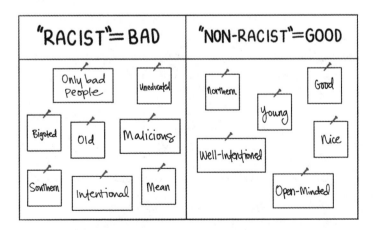

racist" White people who weren't members of the Klan but who weren't stopping the Klan either.

We invite you to move beyond the good/bad binary framework that locks us into a fixed mindset and makes it hard to create change. If racism is something that White people benefit from, then White people need to help change it. Resistance to being seen as bad—especially when one thinks of oneself as a good person—prevents that change.

This is why it can be so hard to talk about racism in our society. Any possibility of being labeled a racist feels like character assassination. If a person is a racist, or even benefits from racism, our habit of binary thinking means they can never be anything else. White people will do anything to avoid being called racist. Because of this, some people have called the word "racist" White-people kryptonite.

Being exposed to the kryptonite of the racist label engenders all kinds of feelings, such as sadness, outrage, confusion, grief, guilt, and shame. Immediately people become defensive. And the defensive posture that White people take in order to avoid being pushed to the "racist" side of the binary makes it nearly impossible to talk about what racism is and how it affects everyone. It makes it impossible to engage in the reflection, receptivity, thoughtfulness, and dialogue that antiracism requires of White people. When we focus on individual self-image, on goodness or badness, we close down the very conversation that could help us confront racism in our society and in ourselves.

The good/bad binary is a false dichotomy. All people hold prejudices, especially across racial lines in a society deeply divided by race.

—Robin

BLATANT or SYSTEMIC?

*During the 2020 presidential campaign I saw a
meme on a social media post that said, "How do
you like your racism, systemic or blatant?" The
word "systemic" was over a picture of Joe Biden.
The word "blatant" was over a picture of Donald
Trump. I commented under the picture that the
formula was wrong. I feel that we must admit
that we all live in a society that is inherently and
systemically racist. Therefore both candidates should
have appeared under the word "systemic." Similarly,
in 2019 many were quick to judge the Democratic
governor of Virginia, Ralph Northam, for photos
that showed him wearing Blackface in college.
That was clearly and blatantly racist. However,
I was much more interested in the policies that he
had shaped in his career as a politician than
in the individual acts that were captured on
camera in his youth. And I was much more
interested in how he responded to the discovery
of the photos with remorse and responsibility,
as well as in the differences that he would make
moving forward. —Toni*

Historian Carol Anderson suggests that systemic racism continues to exist because of "White rage," a term she coined to describe how many White people tend to react when Black people are successful. White rage is resentment of Black advancement. It doesn't look like marching in the streets or yelling in anger—it gets played out in courtrooms, in Congress, on school boards and in local governments.[5] It is a calm and more subtle way in which White people reinforce the racial hierarchy when they are threatened by Black people's achievements. Dr. Anderson writes, "A Black man was elected president of the United States: the ultimate advancement and thus the ultimate affront. Perhaps not surprisingly voting rights were severely curtailed, the federal government was shut down, and more than once the Office of the President was shockingly, openly, and publicly disrespected by other elected officials."[6]

As we talked about in Chapter 3, there is no "non-racism." When White people consider themselves "not racist," they position themselves outside the racial dynamics of US society. Suddenly racism is not their problem, which means they don't have to be part of the solution. But we cannot end racism without White people.

Remember the idea of a common socialization? Because White people get socialized in similar ways, they also respond in similar ways when the topic of racism comes up. Their typical responses emerge from the good/bad binary—as well as from the desire to not be seen as bad. See if any of these expressions sound familiar:

All the statements above come from a desire to lessen the impact of racism, or to position oneself on the "not racist" side of the binary. But the result is to protect the racial status quo by taking race off the table. It's like White people want race not to matter, but all the ways in which they pretend racism is not a problem just make it matter more. How do we actually make race matter less so that people can truly have equality and justice? Well, first, we can examine statements such as these and consider how the very things White people say to show that they are not racist actually end up reinforcing racism.

Dr. Carol Anderson is a professor of African American Studies at Emory University and the author of several books on racial injustice, including *White Rage: The Unspoken Truth of Our Racial Divide*, a *New York Times* best seller and winner of the National Book Critics Circle Award. From growing up worrying about her brother who was serving in Vietnam to watching her neighborhood change into a place the 6 o'clock news would repeatedly describe in negative terms, Professor Anderson understood at an early age that policymakers and activists played a powerful role in shaping society. She set out to find out how they did so and grapple with her own role and influence in challenging racial injustice.[7]

So many of those statements are familiar to me, and not only because I've heard them—but because I've thought them and I've said them! The one I find myself saying a lot references all my Black friends: "Well, my Black friends . . ." I reference my Black friends because I want people to know that I have a diverse social network. But the truth is that I connect more easily with White people. My friendships with Black friends take more work. I'm not sure why, but I think it's because we're both doing something that is more challenging; we're both choosing to be a part of a relationship in which there's potential for misunderstanding, in which we will have to navigate different perspectives on race. On some level I'm afraid this means there's something wrong with me, or I'm bad. So then I end up talking about "my Black friends" to make sure people know I'm not bad. I have to remember that I can't prove my anti-racism by making declarations about my beliefs or convincing people of my diverse reality. It's more impactful if I keep hearing the impact of racism on others—and learning about its impact on me and my behaviors. It's more impactful if I move away from trying to look a certain way and put that energy toward becoming the person I want to be and creating the world I want to live in. —Ali

Some whites are more thoughtful, aware,
and receptive to feedback than others, but
no cross-racial relationship is free from
the dynamics of racism in this society.

—Robin

> When I facilitate groups with my friend Yvonne, she
> always tells our White participants, "If you start
> naming your Black friends and have never had a
> conversation about racism with those people, then
> you don't have a friendship. You just know some
> Black people." —Toni

What follows is an explanation of why the statements shown above are problematic.

"I treat everyone the same."

This statement comes from the desire for racism to have less impact than it does. It comes from a discomfort with racial difference, that is often the result of being taught to be colorblind. It also comes from a fear that if our society tries to fix historical wrongs by giving preferential treatment to People of Color, White people will be disadvantaged. All these responses neglect to see the profound impact of racism throughout history. And furthermore, they neglect the very real fact that people do have different racial, ethnic, and cultural backgrounds. These backgrounds shape the experiences of racism that People of Color have, but they also shape their identities and their communities. Treating everyone the same means ignoring large parts of who People of Color are. It also means ignoring the historical advantage that White people have received from being White. No one actually treats everyone the same. Insisting that we do is unrealistic.

"I go to a very diverse school."

This statement rests on the idea that racists can't go to a diverse school or be near People of Color. But of course, even blatant racists can do so. Going to a diverse school is a great thing. It means you may have more opportunities to develop relationships, understandings, and connections with people who are racially different from you. But it also may not mean that. Many schools are socially segregated by race even within a diverse larger population. Systemic segregation also occurs as a result of academic tracking, where White and Asian American students tend to be tracked into higher-level classes while Black, Latinx, and Indigenous students tend to be tracked into lower-level classes. Beyond that, simply being beside and around People of Color does not mean that White people have authentic cross-racial relationships and connections with them. Attending a diverse school is not evidence of non-racism, and using it as an excuse for not listening and not learning about racism does very little to further anti-racism. But if a White person does attend a racially diverse school, they have the opportunity to connect with and learn from their Peers of Color—if they stay open to learning about their peers' experiences.

"I have People of Color in my family."

When White people have People of Color in their family, they are likely closer to understanding the pain and reality of racism that People of Color have to live with than White people who don't. But those White people should ask themselves, "Have I talked with my Family Members of Color about how racism impacts them, or how it impacts us as a family? Have I asked what I as a White person can do to support them?" Loving someone from another racial group interrupts the prescribed racial status quo in important ways, but it does not change the larger societal dynamic. Many heterosexual cisgender men love hetero cisgender women. Some couples even create gender-equitable parenting, work, and household relationships. But that doesn't mean sexism goes away. In fact, healthy heterosexual relationships often involve an analysis of how sexism fixes certain roles in relationships so that the individuals in the relationship can recognize those roles and challenge them, should they so choose. Healthy cross-racial friendships and relationships do the same with racism.

"My parents campaigned for Obama."

In the horror movie *Get Out*, written and directed by Jordan Peele, the White parents deliver a classic liberal line to demonstrate how woke they are: "I would have voted for Obama for a third term if I could have." If you've seen the movie (spoiler alert if you haven't), you know that those particular White people were deeply invested in demonstrating how much they love Black people so they could win their trust. They needed the trust of Black people so they could use them for nefarious purposes. Although *Get Out* is fictional, it is a stark depiction of how someone can profess a love for Black people while still hurting them. Having voted for Obama—even having campaigned for Obama—did not fix racism. Supporting a Black candidate is not the same thing as supporting Black issues. Supporting a Black person for president does not dismantle systemic racism. People campaigning for Obama did a lot to help US society shift toward electing its first Black president. But the question is not "How did you show up for a few months in 2008 and 2012?" The question is "How do you show up for racial justice today? How will you show up tomorrow?"

"Focusing on race is what divides us."

Many people believe that focusing on race is divisive. This is because they are used to not talking about race and want to maintain the superficial comfort that comes from avoiding difficult conversations. But authentic connections require depth. When we focus on race, we begin to see fractures in our communities that have always been there. This calls us to recognize and challenge racism, rather than deny it. Focusing on race can help us connect more authentically and work for justice in our communities to heal those long-standing fractures. In this way, focusing on race can be more connecting and healing than divisive. If we are paying attention, we know that we are *already* divided by race. Not talking about racism has not changed that. Can you think of any other societal problem that we would say it's best to avoid talking about? Suicide? Sexual assault? Bullying? Eating disorders? Depression? Drug addiction? We know that talking about these issues is an important first step in addressing them. Racism belongs on that list too.

Refusing to engage in authentic exploration of racial realities erases (and denies) alternate racial experiences.

—Robin

Afterthoughts

ACTIVITY

At the end of this chapter we saw responses to several common statements that White people make when they are in the good/bad binary frame of mind. In a small group, practice your own responses to the following statements in a way that practices a both/and mindset rather than a good/bad mindset.

- I don't see color. (Here's an example: I know you say you don't see color because you don't want to judge people based on race, *and* when you say that it denies the reality of so many People of Color.)
- Race doesn't mean anything to me.
- There isn't a prejudiced bone in my body.
- I have Native American ancestry.

Chapter 6

WHY DOES RACISM ALWAYS SEEM SO BLACK AND WHITE?

As we have noted in other chapters, the US is shaped by a racial hierarchy that puts White people at the top and Black people at the bottom, as if they are complete opposites. This is part of why racism often gets superficially confined to a discussion of these two seemingly distinct poles: because they mark the extreme ends of the racial hierarchy. When discussions of racism revolve around Black and White, they're not wrong. They're just incomplete.

We want to begin this chapter by clarifying some of the racial categories. What is race? What is ethnicity? And when do the two overlap? Why are some groups defined by a color (Black, White) while some are defined by a geographic ancestry (Asian American/Pacific Islander) and others by an ethnic identity (Latinx)? When we talk about Native people, is that a racial designation, or something else? After looking at racial groups and the terms used to describe them (as well as which terms to use), we will talk about the different ways that racism impacts different groups. In this chapter you will see how complicated race is, and why our opinions are seldom very informed.

In most news sources and educational literature today, there tend to be five recognized "racial groups" in the US:

- Asian American/Pacific Islander
- Black
- Indigenous/Native
- Latino/Hispanic
- White

In addition to these five major groups, there are the categories of "multiracial," "biracial," and "transracially adopted." The fastest-growing of all the racial groups is actually people who are multiracial or biracial. In the 2010 census, 9 million Americans identified as multiracial. In 2020, 33.8 million Americans identified as multiracial.[1] That's a 275 percent increase! Another way people identify themselves is as transracially adopted or as part of a transracially adoptive family.

Transracially adoptive families are families in which one or more members are adopted and have a different racial group membership from others in the family. People who are transracially adopted may identify with one of the above five "racial groups" but have a unique relationship to that group based on the racial context in which they grew up.

Why Put Quotes Around "Racial Groups"?

We put "racial groups" in quotes because although these groups do exist, they are not biologically real. What does it mean to say that race is not biologically real? It means that race is something humans made up. Sociologists call this a social construct. In other words, there is no biological definition of a Black person, a White person, an Asian American person, a Latinx person, an Indigenous person, etc. To say that someone has a "race" is to assign a categorization that is social and political, not natural or biological. Another thing that is socially constructed is cash. If you gave me a twenty-dollar bill and asked for change, you'd be disappointed if I handed you back a one-dollar bill. I could make the argument that we were exchanging one bill for another bill—it's an even trade. But since we have a socially agreed upon contract that a twenty-dollar bill is worth twenty one-dollar bills, my argument would be unacceptable. When enough people agree on something in a society, the social construction gets more widely used. Credit, checks, and now cryptocurrencies like Bitcoin all had to be introduced slowly so that people could come to agree on their meaning and the legitimacy of their value. As we consider how to challenge racism, we have to keep working to undo our collective idea that race is biologically real.

> **Melanin** is a naturally occurring pigment that gives human beings their skin color, hair color, and eye color.
>
> **DEFINITION**

Sometimes the names of racial groups are capitalized, sometimes they're not. Some choose to capitalize words like "White" and "Black" to distinguish them from literal colors. Nobody is literally the color white of this page or literally the color black of the print in this book, but they might have an identity defined by those racial labels. Racial labels are not literal biological categories, but rather, as described above, social and political (sociopolitical) categories. They are social because they are understood, used, and reinforced by the people and society around you. They are political with a small p because they are often defined and enforced by the government, including on the census, in court cases, in policy, and on official documents.

What's the difference between race and ethnicity?

According to the Association of American Anthropologists (AAA), race is "a recent idea created by western Europeans . . . to account for differences among people and justify colonization, conquest, enslavement, and social hierarchy among humans. The term is used to refer to groupings of people according to common origin or background and associated with perceived biological markers."[2] The AAA defines ethnicity as "an idea similar to race that groups people according to common origin or background. The term usually refers to social, cultural, religious, linguistic, and other affiliations although, like race, it is sometimes linked to perceived biological markers. Ethnicity is often characterized by cultural features, such as dress, language, religion, and social organization."

Religion is often included as an aspect of ethnicity, but it is also a separate category from race and ethnicity. Consider a person who identifies as Black, Muslim, and Arab. These three identities are connected but distinct. Black is that person's race, Islam is their religion, and Arab is their ethnicity. Similarly, a person who identifies as White, Catholic, and Italian has a race, a religion, and an ethnicity that overlap and are connected but are still distinct categories. However, there is a difference in how each of these hypothetical people will be responded to and treated in the United States. Because Catholicism is a mainstream Christian religion, people in the US don't tend to experience discrimination for wearing a cross or displaying other religious markers. But religious markers that are racialized, like hijabs for Muslims, turbans for Sikhs, or kippas for Jews, put people who wear them at risk of being targeted with violence or discrimination. Particularly after September 11, 2001, harassment and violence increased against people who were *perceived* as Muslims; this included not only Muslim people, but also most Brown people, Sikhs, and Arab Americans who were not Muslim.

How Do You Know Which Term to Use?

Yeah, but... **which terms do I use? All this terminology is confusing.**

When referring to a person's racial or ethnic background, try whenever possible to use the terminology and identity that they themselves prefer. Be as accurate as possible; it might take practice, especially if you're not used to the terminology. W. E. B. Du Bois said that race is a double-edged sword that both gives us our identities and takes them away. A person might derive meaning, connection, and community from their racial group designation. But they also get their individuality erased when people see them first (and only) as a part of their racial group. Don't take away someone's identity by imposing a racial designation on them. Find out how people choose to identify, and honor that identification.

Remember that when race is confusing, that's because it is not a straightforward concept. If you don't know the words for things, that's because the words and their meanings are constantly changing and evolving. There are probably words in this book whose meanings have shifted since we wrote it. Over the course of your lifetime, the preferred terms will change for different people and different groups. Again, remember to ask people how they identify, and honor their self-identity. If it doesn't make sense to ask directly, listen for what they say.

Here is a summary of some of the broad ways that people might identify:

SOUTH ASIAN · INDIGENOUS · LATINO · AFRO-LATINX · TRANSRACIALLY ADOPTED · PERSIAN

ABORIGINAL · ASIAN · PACIFIC ISLANDER · WHITE · HISPANIC · MIDDLE EASTERN

BLACK · FIRST NATION · MULTIRACIAL · BIPOC · THE GLOBAL MAJORITY · ASIAN AMERICAN

LATINX · BIRACIAL · ALASKA NATIVE · LATINA · EUROPEAN AMERICAN · AFRICAN CARIBBEAN

AFRICAN AMERICAN · NATIVE AMERICAN · CONTINENTAL AFRICAN · ARAB · PEOPLE OF COLOR · DESI AMERICAN

- Black, African American, Afro Caribbean, Continental African, African
- White, European American, Euro-American, Anglo-American
- Latino/Latina/Latinx, Afro-Latinx, Indigenous, Hispanic
- Asian American, Asian, Desi-American, South Asian, Southeast Asian, East Asian, Pacific Islander
- Indigenous, Native American, Alaska Native, First Nations, Aboriginal
- Persian, Arab, Middle Eastern
- Biracial or multiracial
- BIPOC (Black, Indigenous, People of Color), Person/ People of Color, BBIA (Black, Brown, Indigenous, Asian), the Global Majority

Black

Black is a racial group that sometimes gets called African American. But Black and African American are not the same thing. Black is a category that tends to encompass African Americans but also includes people who are recently immigrated from Africa or the Caribbean—that is, people who have ancestors in Africa but whose ancestors were not enslaved in the United States. When people identify as African American, it usually means they are part of a group of Americans who are descended from Africans who were enslaved in the US. Contrary to what many non-Black people think, the terms "African American" and "Black" are not interchangeable. Many African Americans identify as Black, too, but many Black people in the US do not identify as African American.

Yeah, but... **if a person is White and from South Africa, but then moves to the US, aren't they technically African American?**

Yeah . . . no. In the same way that White people are not literally white (more pinkish, really), and in the same way that Black people are not literally black (more brownish, really), African American is not a literal category. Again, it's a sociopolitical category. African American is a form of ethnicity. It is a particular group with a history and identity, with many particular cultural and linguistic styles. A White person who is from South Africa and now lives in the US is an immigrant, a South African, and perhaps also (depending on immigration status) an American. But they are not "African American."

Polls show that most African Americans prefer the term "Black," but it's always best to ask or honor a person's preference.

> *How do I identify? It means a lot to me when people are intentional about the way they refer to my race. Often people will use the term "African American," which has been a respectful term for people who look like me. Because of that, I want people to say "African American" first, and then I want to give them permission to say "Black." In actuality, I primarily identify myself as Black. Is that too confusing? It's confusing to me too.* —Toni

Latinx/Hispanic

Latinx/Hispanic is a category that encompasses people who have ancestry in Latin America. It is sometimes treated as a racial group and sometimes treated as an ethnicity. The US census even separates Hispanic as a distinct ethnicity, asking people first to identify *racially* and then to identify as Hispanic or non-Hispanic (ethnically). So a person could be ethnically Hispanic while being racially either White or Black. But many Latinx (pronounced "luh-TEE-neks") people don't identify as White or Black. Many Latinx people have multiracial families, where they witness how racism impacts different family members depending on the lightness or darkness of their skin. In much of the academic literature on race, as well as in the ways that racial issues or disparities are reported in the news, Latinx is treated as another racial category, similar to Black or White.

Some Latinx activists take issue with the term "Hispanic," which technically means "of Spain," because it defines a group's identity by the power of Spain, which colonized Mexico, Central America, and parts of South America. In an effort to resist being named by the conquering power, they began using the term "Latino" (now sometimes "Latinx").

"Hispanic" is also sometimes resisted because it is a government term that suggests bureaucratic categorization, rather than unity or identity.

Why the *X*?

In Spanish, "Latino" with an *o* is the gender all-encompassing term. But the traditional forms of making an adjective masculine (Latino) or feminine (Latina) reinforce a gender binary. For this reason, many people have stopped using the male form (Latino) as a general catch-all category and have changed to using Latinx. Not all Latinx people use this term or even know it. In fact, 40 percent of Latinos surveyed said they don't identify with the term Latinx, and 30 percent said that use of the term would make them less likely to vote for the candidate who used it.[3] How Latinx people choose to identify in terms of language preference—as is true of people of all racial and ethnic backgrounds—is up to each individual.

In the novel *Americanah*, by Chimamanda Ngozi Adichie, a Nigerian student named Ifemelu comes to the US to study and develops a blog in which she writes about race. She struggles with understanding the category "Hispanic." Here is a quote from the part of the book where she is learning what it means to be Hispanic:

If she [Ifemelu] had met Alma in Nigeria, she would have thought of her as white, but she would learn that Alma was Hispanic, an American category that was, confusingly, both an ethnicity and a race, and she would remember Alma when, years later, she wrote a blog post titled "Understanding America for the Non-American Black: What Hispanic Means."

Hispanic means the frequent companions of American blacks in poverty rankings, Hispanic means a

slight step above American blacks in the race lad-
der, Hispanic means the chocolate-skinned woman
from Peru, Hispanic means the indigenous people of
Mexico. Hispanic means the biracial-looking folks
from the Dominican Republic. Hispanic means the
paler folks from Puerto Rico. Hispanic also means the
blond, blue-eyed guy from Argentina. All you need to
be is Spanish-speaking but not from Spain and voila,
you're a race called Hispanic.[4]

In Lin-Manuel Miranda's Broadway musical and movie *In
the Heights*, the character Carla expresses her Latina identity
like this: "My mom is Dominican Cuban. My dad is from
Chile and PR, which means I'm Chile-Domini-Curican. . . .
But I always say I'm from Queens!"[5]

Because of the broad range of skin colors among Latinx
people, racial categories can be extra confusing for people
who count themselves in this group. As racial-identity scholars Ferdman and Gallegos have noted, "Latinos have had an
uneasy relationship with prevailing racial constructs in the
U.S. These 'either/or' notions, typically Black/White or White/
not White, have not easily incorporated or allowed for the
polychromatic (that is, multicolored) reality of Latinos."[6]

Asian American

Like all racial categories, Asian American is a problematic
category. It includes people whose ancestors come from
vastly different countries that today encompass almost five
billion people. Further, Asian Americans have a wide variety of economic backgrounds—and, like White and Black
people, a large variation in how long their ancestors have
been in the US. Using one racial designation for people who
have immigrated from an immense geographic area over

multiple generations leads to a category that many people who fall within it don't necessarily identify with. A Korean American person might have ancestral conflict with a Japanese American person, but in the US their descendants get put into the same category: Asian American. There is a common assumption that people who "look Asian" must be recent immigrants, or the children of immigrants, rather than Americans descended from Americans descended from Americans, as so many Asian Americans are. Throughout US history, Asian Americans have been treated as second-class citizens, such as when Japanese Americans were imprisoned in camps during World War II. Only a fraction of German Americans were imprisoned at that time, in spite of the fact that the US was at war with Germany as well.

Asian Americans include people with ancestry in China, Hong Kong, Singapore, Laos, Cambodia, Myanmar, Malaysia, East Timor, Mongolia, South Korea, North Korea, the Philippines, Taiwan, Vietnam, Japan, Indonesia, Thailand, and the Pacific Islands. Asian Americans also include Hmong people and Karen people, whose roots are in many different nations. People who have ancestral ties to South Asian countries, like India, Pakistan, Bangladesh, Afghanistan, Nepal, and Sri Lanka, are also Asian American. People who are of South Asian descent may identify as Desi or Desi American or South Asian or Pakistani American or Nepalese American, Bangla, or Bengali American. But again, this category is so vast and so complex that it is crucial to ask individuals how they self-identify, rather than assuming they relate to the pan-Asian category known as Asian American.

Native People

Many Native people do not tend to identify as People of Color, although most certainly identify as people impacted by white supremacy. For most Native people, it's not just racism but also colonization that has undermined their humanity, their way of life, their sovereignty. Racism is a part of colonization.

Being a Native person may mean that a person has official tribal status, but many people in the US identify as Native and do not have official tribal citizenship. One's tribal citizenship is a legal—not cultural or racial—identity. Tribal citizenship is a nationality, providing for unique political status in US law.

Sometimes you will hear Native people referred to as "Indigenous." Similar to the term "Native," this means that they and their ancestors are from this land as far back as can be recorded. They are the only group that is indigenous—or original—to the Americas. Everyone else here, or their ancestors, either immigrated or was forced to come. "Indigenous" is also used to refer to groups of people across the globe who are indigenous to their lands, including the Aboriginal people of Australia, the Quechua people of South America, the Mayan or Nahua people of Central America, and the Hill Tribes of Bangladesh, to name a few.

Many Native people will say that rather than being called Native or Indigenous, whenever possible they would like to be introduced using their tribal affiliations. There are 574 federally recognized tribal nations in the US today.[7] An act of solidarity for non-Native Americans would be to learn the names of many of these nations, including the ones in your area. Many tribal nations remain unrecognized by the federal government. To learn more, check out the website run by the National Congress of American Indians.[8]

Many Native people prefer that non-Native people avoid using the term "Indian." "Indian" is sometimes used as an in-group term among Native people or in more established (older) organizations, such as the Smithsonian National

Museum of the American Indian, Indian Health Services, the American Indian Library Association, or the National Congress of American Indians (referenced above). The term was given to the inhabitants of what we now refer to as America by the Europeans who colonized the land. They assumed in their travels across the Atlantic Ocean that they had reached the shores of India, which is how they came to erroneously call Native people Indians. Although the term has been debunked, it has historical and cultural meaning to some Native people, who may use it to describe their own identity or group.

White

White people are people descended from Europeans, a category that has broadened in the twentieth century to include people from Great Britain, Western Europe, Eastern Europe, Russia, and beyond, including European and Ashkenazi Jews. The reality is that many People of Color have some European ancestry too. But being White has historically meant not *also* having heritage from other racial backgrounds. In order to create the illusion of an elite status, Whiteness was mythologized to have a purity that would be "polluted" with as little as "one drop of blood" from another racial group, especially from Black people. This was called the law of hypodescent.[9] It essentially stated that if a person had one Black ancestor, for example, then they were Black, no matter the actual color of their skin. Different states treated hypodescent differently, but by and large, having even just a single Black ancestor made a person Black, whereas a White person could only be White if they were descended exclusively from people considered to be White. Again, this theory of what it took to maintain pure Whiteness was made up. There's no such thing as racial purity. You cannot "pollute" a bloodline. All human

beings have blood, DNA, and different amounts of melanin, and there's no evidence that people are more similar to
people in their own racial groups than people in other racial
groups. In fact, biologists have shown that people often have
more in common genetically with people outside their racial
groups than within.[10]

Some readers may have heard the term "Caucasian" used
to refer to White people. Many people don't know that this
term has racist origins. It refers to people from the Caucasus
Mountains region, where Europe and Asia intersect. Johann
Blumenbach coined the word "Caucasian" in 1795 when he
created a five-part hierarchy of human types based on skulls
that he studied. He called the skull from the Caucasus region
the "most beautiful form of the skull, from which others
diverge."[11] The study of skull shapes was a branch of pseu-
doscience called phrenology that has been widely debunked.
Blumenbach's hierarchy of human types became the foundation for eugenics, which is the science of controlling population growth by sterilizing, relocating, or eliminating "less
desirable" people, as the Nazis did during the Holocaust
to people who were Jewish, Romani, queer, disabled, and
Jehovah's Witnesses,[12] and as the apartheid regime did to
Black Africans, Coloured people, and sometimes Indian
people in South Africa.

"Caucasian" is not an accurate term for White people;
very few White people in the US today have ancestry in the
Caucasus Mountains. Perhaps most importantly, it is not the
term used by US law. Throughout US history, White people
have been described as "white" in legal documents and decisions.[13] That is why we use this term as we try to understand
the impact of "White" as a racial category.

Many White people do not want to identify as White
because they aren't used to being categorized by others as
members of a racial group, instead of just "people" or just

"normal." But as the conversation about race and racism becomes more mainstream, Whiteness is being named more often. In turn, White people are starting to hear themselves labeled as a member of a group. It can be awkward and uncomfortable. But it is also a great first step toward racial self-awareness and challenging the idea that some people are "normal" and others are not. If we don't have the words to name something, then we can't talk about it.

Multiracial

Multiracial people are those who have parents or ancestry from more than one racial group. For example, a woman who is both Black and Latina might identify as Afro-Latina. But for people who are biracial or multiracial, there can be multiple different ways to identify. According to racial-identity scholar Maria Root, biracial and multiracial people may identify in any of the following ways at different times in their lives:

1. feet in both groups
2. shifting identity based on context
3. holding an extra-racial identity by deconstructing race or opting out of identification in the US racial categories
4. sitting on the border
5. creating a home in one camp and foraying into another camp[14]

People of Color

The term "People of Color" was created to describe people who were previously referred to as "non-White." The goal was to devise a term that described all people who were negatively impacted by racism in a way that could lead to greater solidarity across groups.[15] "Non-White" was replaced because it described people according to what they were not, rather than what they were.

> **People of Color**, as a group, includes all people who are not defined or perceived as White. This includes multiracial people, biracial people, Black people, Latinx people, Asian American people, Indigenous people, and many others who might not fit neatly into any of those racial categories.
>
> **DEFINITION**

"People of Color" is now sometimes replaced with the term "BIPOC," which stands for Black, Indigenous, and People of Color. Another term for People of Color is the "Global Majority," which recognizes that although People of Color may be a racial minority in the US, they are part of a majority around the world.

"BBIA," a term we just learned, means "Black, Brown, Indigenous, Asian." As we've said, the terminology shifts regularly. Terms like BIPOC and BBIA honor the fact that Indigenous people also experience racial oppression, like other groups of People of Color. But in other ways these group-lumping terms can dishonor the political identities of Native people as members of nations by making it seem as though racism and colonialism are the same experience. Colonialism—sometimes called settler colonialism—is the historical and current process of "remov[ing] and eras[ing] Indigenous people in order to take the land for use by settlers in perpetuity."[16] White supremacy is at the heart of both colonialism and racism, but they are different processes with distinct impacts.

Race Is Made Up . . . but Racism Is Real

If race isn't real, then why can't we just stop talking about it? Even though race is a made-up concept, racism is a real phenomenon that has a significant impact on people's lives. We cannot change it if we don't talk about it.

To address the topic of this chapter head on, why does talk of race and racism often seem only black and white? When race gets discussed in our society historically, it's about Black people, because we have set up black and white as complete opposites—the two far ends of a continuum. Whiteness is the end of the continuum that we don't name, which reinforces the myth that it is the "normal" or "superior" end. But white supremacy is at the root of racism against *all* groups of People of Color and Native people, not only Black people. Latinx people and Asian Americans are impacted by racism too. In this section, we will delineate some of the distinct ways that racism affects different racial groups.

Racism Against Latinx People

The racial group Latino/Latina/Latinx includes people who have recently immigrated to the US as well as people whose families have been in the country since the US forcibly incorporated the lands of their ancestors. The states we now call Texas, Utah, Nevada, New Mexico, California, and Arizona, as well as the western part of Colorado, were once actually part of Mexico. But following the Mexican-American War, the US took over those lands and their people. As some people say, they didn't cross the border—the border crossed them. Bigotry that tells Latinx citizens they do not belong in the US forgets this history. Policy and discrimination that treats Latinx immigrants to the US as inferior or illegal underlie anti-Latinx racism. Laws and policies that criminalize or punish the use of Spanish or that prevent schools from teaching Latinx heritage are part of the effort to alienate Latinx people from their cultures, histories, and identities.

The US military has a long history of interfering in the politics of Latin American countries. US policy has played a role in destabilizing some Latin American nations by supporting coups or engaging in other military interventions in order to protect US economic interests.[17] The resulting instability often forced citizens of those countries to immigrate to the US in search of safety and economic opportunity. This is part of what creates Latinx immigration to the United States today. The dependence of the US on the relatively inexpensive labor of undocumented immigrants is part of what feeds the disinterest in changing our immigration system. The use of the term "illegal alien" is meant to dehumanize and criminalize undocumented immigrants so they are not seen as worthy of respect and empathy, political rights, or a minimum wage. If you need to refer to someone who is undocumented, it is more affirming to use the term "undocumented immigrant" rather than "illegal alien." Human beings cannot be illegal.

Microaggressions (see the definition box) against Latinx people include the stereotypes that come out on Cinco de Mayo, a holiday that many Americans celebrate in a formulaic manner by drinking alcohol, eating salsa, and wearing sombreros—as if all Latinx people were Mexican, and as if that were the sum total of Mexican culture. They come out in the jokes about Spanglish in which Americans incorporate corrupted versions of Spanish into daily life or mock Spanish-language accents, as in the popular children's book series *Skippyjon Jones*. Latinx people have also experienced some of the same racism that is typically directed at Black people, including redlining, denial of home loans, barriers to voting, military veterans being denied treatment equal to that of White veterans, and assumptions of guilt from law enforcement.[18] These are some of the ways that racism shows up against Latinx people.

Anti-Asian Racism

There are many accounts of when Asian Americans first came to the US. According to Ronald Takaki, some of the first Chinese migrants arrived in San Francisco in 1849,[20] about twelve years before the start of the Civil War, which marked the beginning of the end of slavery. Russell Shorto, a historian and author of *The Island at the Center of the World*, writes of Asian Americans in New York City in the 1700s. The book *1421: The Year China Discovered America*, by Gavin Menzies, makes a compelling argument for Chinese explorers having arrived in what is now the US as early as 1421, seventy-one years before Columbus landed in what is now the Bahamas. All these narratives point to different parts of a larger story: "Asian American" as a group is not made up exclusively of immigrants who came to this country after 1965, when the government passed the Immigration and Nationality Act.

Asian Americans have been in the US since there has been a US. The story of Asian Americans is often left out of history curricula. This erasure is itself a form of racism.[21]

In the wake of COVID-19, violence against Asian American people has increased. People of all different types of Asian heritage have been attacked. While this spike in anti-Asian violence is tied to people's unjustified fears and bigotry, anti-Asian racism is persistent, encompassing racial microaggressions that have endured over time. The following is a list of microaggressions faced by Asian Americans. It was compiled by Derald Wing Sue and his research team, based on extensive interviews and surveys:[22]

- seeing Asian Americans as aliens in their own land
- assuming or believing that Asian people are more intelligent than other people
- denying that Asian Americans experience racism
- exoticizing Asian American women
- invalidating differences between Asian American people from different ethnic and national backgrounds—that is, assuming all Asian Americans speak Chinese or are from the same place
- pathologizing cultural values/communication styles
- treating Asian American people as not "real" Americans, or as second-class citizens
- invisibilizing Asian Americans by failing to see their contributions or failing to include them in US history, culture, and identity

Other ways that anti-Asian racism shows up in schools includes imitating Asian accents, making fun of facial features, not learning how to pronounce names, saying that certain Asian foods smell bad, or assuming all Asian people know martial arts or are good at math.

> WHILE WHITENESS AND BLACKNESS ARE CONSTRUCTED AS THE TWO FACES OF AMERICA, ASIANS AND ASIAN AMERICANS HAVE HISTORICALLY BEEN SITUATED AS PERPETUAL FOREIGNERS.

STACEY LEE

Dr. Stacey J. Lee is a Chinese American professor of educational policy studies at the University of Wisconsin-Madison. Her research centers around race, class, and gender. Lee is the author of *Up Against Whiteness: Race, School, and Immigrant Youth* (the source of the above quote) and *Unraveling the Model Minority Stereotype: Listening to Asian American Youth*. Her most recent article, cowritten with colleagues, is titled "'Asians for Black Lives, Not Asians for Asians': Building Southeast Asian American and Black Solidarity."

Professor of educational policy studies Stacey J. Lee studies how white supremacy requires assimilation of immigrants for success and belonging in US society. Lee describes assimilation like this: "To be considered 'good,' immigrants must aspire to and show the likelihood of achieving middle-class status and in other ways assimilate to the dominant White culture. Poor immigrants who want to achieve upward mobility in mainstream American society often interpret the racial conditions to mean that they must simultaneously reembrace whiteness and reject blackness. Embracing whiteness, however, does not mean that the status of whiteness is in fact available to non-Whites."[23] In other words, although immigrant Students of Color feel pressure to assimilate into Whiteness, they can never *be* White because they don't *appear* White. This makes the demand to fit in with Whiteness all the more confusing, frustrating, and unfair.

The pressure to assimilate impacts Native people too, as we will see, to be as much like the dominant (White) culture as possible, in language, culture, dress, presentation, values, worldview, etc. As the scholar Lee Anne Bell has written, this process of assimilation "has justified the near extermination of Native people on this continent."[24]

Native People and Colonization

One of the most prominent forms of racism that Native people experience is that of erasure. Many non-Native people learn about Native people as if they only lived in the past and are no longer here. Native communities continue to experience the ramifications of displacement and violence that we learn about from history books, including the legacy of boarding schools, which operated from 1869 to the 1960s.[25] In boarding schools, Native children were reprimanded, abused, forced to live in subhuman conditions, and even killed for using their language or adhering to their culture. The stated goal of these schools was to "kill the Indian to save the man"—that is, to take away their culture and anything about them that was Indian.[26]

Native identity itself remains under assault from Western culture. Most US public schools embrace an understanding of mainstream history that minimizes or erases the genocide of Native people and tells the story of the US—including naming wars, places, and landmarks—from the perspective and in the language of the settler colonizers. This history also contradicts the realities and histories of Native people who belong to sovereign nations within the US. Although most Native people are US citizens, many are also simultaneously members of sovereign tribal nations that have separate and distinct governing bodies from the US government. These nations maintain that much of the land settled by the US was never formally sold, given, or otherwise handed over to the US. The term for this is "unceded territory."

The histories and politics of the 574 recognized tribal nations across the country differ widely. But Native American people continue to work to maintain their cultures, languages, and sovereignty still today. Most of the boarding schools that tried to destroy Native cultures have been closed, and the efforts to revive those cultures persist, even in the face of unrelenting demands for assimilation. In the practice of assimilation, Native children who continue to embrace Native values, for example, are downgraded for not blending in with a White worldview. If you have ever read the history of how poorly Native people in the US were treated and wished you could have done something, know that the struggle continues to this day, and that allies of all racial backgrounds are needed. Native-led environmental movements are a part of these efforts. Check out the Keep It in the Ground campaign of the Indigenous Environmental

Network,[27] and the Stop the Line 3 Pipeline Campaign[28] for more information.

> *I opened a history textbook recently and turned to the authors' page. Before me were ten White authors. Not just one or two, but ten! Which of those ten people understands the experience of People of Color and Indigenous people? I respect their scholarship; however, there's no way that the textbook was not written from a White point of view.* —Toni

Anti-Blackness

Because all People of Color experience racism in different ways, anti-Blackness describes the specific ways that racism impacts Black people. But beyond that, it describes the painful, prevalent attitude in the US that things associated with Black people are inferior. This tends to include but is not limited to neighborhoods, schools, language, music, literature, and more. The history of anti-Blackness is at the root of the formation of this country, and it is not something that will be easily changed. This is another reason why people often talk about racism in terms of black and white. Black is positioned as the opposite of white, so it is the ultimate "inferior" group; there cannot be a good or better group without a bad or worse group. In this way, the system of racism depends on the unequal relationship *specifically* between White and Black people.

Anti-Blackness is embedded in language that associates darkness with bad and lightness with good; it shows up in White standards of beauty for hair, body type, and skin tone. It includes mass incarceration of Black people who are unfairly prosecuted, and police murders of unarmed Black people. It includes a health care system where racism has been well-documented.[29] It includes systematic exclusion of Black people from housing markets—and even from popular culture awards such as the Emmys (e.g., #EmmysSoWhite).

More and more people are starting to be able to name and expose anti-Blackness. More and more Black people are able to reveal the full complexity of their lives in TV shows, movies, and literature, whether or not non-Black people like it. But it is going to take much more to dismantle anti-Blackness.

Anti-Blackness is visible in the way that US society repeatedly holds Black people back from political and economic success. Racial violence toward Black people and Black communities increases when Black people thrive. Mob violence and attacks of the past, like the Tulsa Race Massacre, did not just destroy Black communities but also extinguished the possibility of passing wealth on to future generations.

TULSA RACE MASSACRE

In 1921, mobs of White people in Tulsa, Oklahoma, demolished Black-owned stores, businesses, and homes, and attacked Black residents of the Greenwood District. This neighborhood, well known for its successful and affluent Black residents, was sometimes referred to as Black Wall Street. Violence erupted over thirty-five blocks. An estimated eight-hundred-plus people were injured, and many were killed in a battle that lasted for over twenty-four hours.[30]

For all who are reading this book (Black and non-Black), it is important to question your own anti-Blackness. Anti-Blackness is not something that most people are conscious of. And it is not something only White people absorb (although it was White people who originated it and continue to uphold it through control of institutions). It's so deeply embedded that everyone absorbs it, including Black people themselves. Many people avoid Black neighborhoods or schools—having been taught to believe that those areas are inferior or unsafe. People are socialized not to question such beliefs or to see them as biases that are embedded in anti-Blackness.

> *It's not only White people who are taught anti-Blackness. Any Person of Color—including Black people—can learn anti-Blackness. I've seen Black students refuse to consider an HBCU (Historically Black College or University) because they believe that a PWI (Predominantly White Institution) is better. I've known Black people who won't go into predominantly Black communities. The power of anti-Blackness as it has been cultivated in the US is that strong. —Toni*

In the white mind, Black people are the ultimate racial "other," and we must grapple with this relationship, for it is a foundational aspect of racial socialization.

—Robin

Where Does Anti-Blackness Come From?

Anti-Blackness is rooted in misinformation, lies, myths, and lack of historical knowledge.

From the start of US history, the maintenance of a clear separation between Black and White people was critical to maintaining the system of enslavement. The rights for each group had to be clearly delineated. There needed to be incentives for White indentured servants to identify more closely with the landowning White men than with enslaved Africans. As Isabel Wilkerson has written, a robust caste system had to be put in place to ensure the separation of White from Black. Marriage across racial lines was strictly prohibited until the Supreme Court deemed this prohibition unconstitutional in the *Loving v. Virginia* court case on June 12, 1967.[31]

Well into the twentieth century, the caste system insisted that the sharing of spaces between Black people and White people would contaminate White people. Beliefs like this led not only to segregation but to seeing Black people as a "poison," threatening the supposed "purity" of Whiteness.

All of this required that White people cut off empathy or feelings of connection they might have had toward Black people. Wilkerson writes, "[The racial caste system] makes it less likely that someone in the dominant caste will have a personal stake in the happiness, fulfillment, or well-being of anyone deemed beneath them or personally identify with them or their plight."[32]

The unconscious anti-Blackness that so many people carry means that when our systems benefit White people or disadvantage Black people, we don't question them. We assume things are the way they are because of an inherent problem with Black people. The very anti-Blackness that so many White people are unconscious of is what makes the oppression of Black people appear rational and even, perhaps, necessary. Anti-Blackness shows up in our systems in some of the following ways.

Schools
- Black children being perceived and punished as though they are older than they really are
- Black children being suspended from school at higher rates than non-Black children, for the same infractions

Housing
- Redlining in neighborhoods
- "White flight" to suburban neighborhoods
- Racially restrictive housing covenants (i.e., if you buy this house, you cannot sell it to Black people)

Criminal Justice
- The school-to-prison pipeline
- Mass incarceration
- The opioid crisis, in which White users receive treatment, versus the crack epidemic, in which Black users were imprisoned

When do feelings of anti-Blackness arise in White people and in other non-Black People of Color? Such feelings can arise whenever people feel threatened, excluded, or outnumbered by Black people, which might happen anytime. So, for example, when they unexpectedly encounter a Black person, when they are in an elevator with Black people, when a group of Black people is sitting together (like in a school cafeteria) even though most of the rest of the room is White, when their Black colleagues go out to eat together as a group, or when a Black person starts to do well in a sport or a field that was stereotypically dominated by White people.

Yeah, but... **we had a Black president!**

The election of Barack Obama in 2008 seemed to some to be a turning point for the US. However, no other president experienced the amount of disrespect, often from other politicians, than President Obama did. This meant that it was actually harder for President Obama to enact policies that were good for Black people than it might have been had he been White. Beyond that, having one Black person in the highest office does not mean that racial equality has been achieved. Look at the backlash to his eight years in office that manifested in the overtly racist political campaigns that followed in 2016. Look at the racial makeup of Congress during his tenure. This is an example of what we mean when we say that racism is prejudice joined with power. The people sitting at the tables of power determine whether and how the systems change. One president is not sufficient to shift those systems.

Afterthoughts

DISCUSSION

With a small group of people, discuss the ways that racism shows up differently for different races of people in the United States.

Chapter 7

SO WHAT EXACTLY IS WHITE FRAGILITY?

Let's review:

- In Chapter 1, we learned why talking about race is so hard for White people. They are unpracticed. They are taught not to.
- In Chapter 2, we established that racism is not just the KKK or a racial slur spray-painted on a wall somewhere. It's systemic, it's historical, and it impacts everyone.
- In Chapter 3, we talked about non-racism, or rather, we pointed out that non-racism is not actually a thing. Non-racism means doing nothing, which means continuing to uphold and collude with a racist system.
- In Chapter 4, we discussed how deeply White people's lives are shaped by being White, such that they don't see themselves as having race, and they grow accustomed to segregation, to not needing to navigate racial stress, to seeing society—and everyone in it—through a White lens.
- In Chapter 5, we talked about how to unlearn racism, starting with unlearning either/or (binary) thinking. When White people are able to take feedback on

their racism—some of which they learned without even knowing it—they can begin to be anti-racist. The r-word (racism) is White-people kryptonite, meaning it automatically weakens a White person's capacity to deal with racism when they get so caught up in defending against it.

- In Chapter 6, we learned about different racial groups and how racism looks different for each of them.

It is clear that there are many factors that cumulatively explain why it can be so hard for a White person to understand racism. Fortunately, understanding all those factors means that a person can begin to confront and unlearn them. Not understanding them is what leads to white fragility.

> When I try to tell a White colleague that something she did hurt me, she puts up her hands as if in defense. When I try to share some of my experiences of racism, she does the same. Eventually it seems like every time she sees me coming, she has her hands up, as if to say, "I give up" or "You caught me" or "It wasn't me" or "I would never do that." I'm never quite sure what she's trying to say, but it's clear that there's literally a physical barrier between us, preventing us from connecting. —Toni

Yeah, but... why *White* Fragility? Aren't People of Color fragile too?

White fragility as a concept is not meant to portray White people as vulnerable or breakable. It's about oversensitivity backed by power, which makes it more like broken glass. It can actually be a form of bullying. It's like saying, "I'm going to make it so miserable for you to challenge me on my beliefs or actions that I bully you into silence about race." It is seldom conscious or intentional, but it still has this impact. This is really different from the more common use of the term "fragile," which suggests a vulnerability or delicacy. As we discussed in Chapter 1, we encourage readers to think about how this kind of bullying backed by power might manifest for you as a person with male privilege or heterosexual privilege. Whiteness is only one particular form of privilege.

White fragility gives a name to something that People of Color have seen for a long time: the defensive rejection that White people often display when asked to see, to talk about, and to reckon with the way racism shapes them—as well as how they perpetuate it. It's meant to describe how White people are unpracticed and untrained at navigating racial stress. They might unconsciously put up their hands and push people away, as Toni's colleague did in the example above, out of a physical sense that they cannot handle the truth about racism. We believe that the more people understand these dynamics, the better equipped they will be to deal with them.

Why does learning about racism feel threatening to White people?

This may come as a surprise, but White people receive a certain amount of protection from being White. If you are a Person of Color and you've experienced the vulnerability of living in a nation that does not always guarantee your safety—or living with a police force or an immigration authority that questions your belonging or your innocence—you already know this. But if you are White, the safety you gain from being White in a racial hierarchy that puts White people at the top means you don't have to worry that the police will stop you *just because* you are White.

> *In the predominantly White suburb where I grew up, we always joked that the police had nothing to do. The only time I interacted with police was when my father got pulled over for speeding or they dropped off the street barriers for our block party. I thought of police as friendly, as helpful. If I ever needed something, I knew I would call the police.* —Ali

Ali's example of feeling safe with police is a literal example of the kind of general racial safety White people feel in the US that many People of Color do not feel. There's safety and comfort in being White, but only if one doesn't challenge the system that grants them safety and comfort. Once a White person starts to challenge that system, they begin to feel a fraction of the vulnerability that People of Color feel on a daily basis, not only in interactions with police but in English class with a White teacher and a White lens on literature, or at the drugstore with a White manager following them to make sure they're not stealing anything.

The racial comfort that White people experience daily means that White people are less able to tolerate even basic levels of racial stress. Think of it as lifting weights to build muscle and improve fitness. The capacity to handle racial stress is built over time, just like weightlifting requires practice, drills, eating nutrient-dense foods, and drinking lots of water. It can't happen in a day; it requires regular practice for years. The capacity to withstand racial stress is a skill any person can develop—but it requires ongoing training, openness, and education. And it involves more than just learning about racism. It also involves *unlearning* the ideologies that hold Whiteness in place. Racial stress is caused by challenges to ideologies like colorblindness and meritocracy. When these ideologies are challenged, there is often an emotional defensive reaction.

Why are White people so defensive about the mere suggestion that they benefit from the racist system in our society? Why does it cause so much racial stress? Let's summarize some of the reasons that we have mentioned so far in this book:

- It is taboo to talk openly about race.
- The good/bad binary makes people think that if they admit to racism, that means they are bad.
- They may hold subtle or unaware fear of or resentment toward People of Color.
- They experience guilt for not acknowledging things about racism.
- They often hold a sense of internalized superiority.
- They are invested in this system, which feels normal, comfortable, and benefits them.
- There is a deep legacy of anti-Black sentiment.
- Racism is not typically seen as a White-people problem.

This defensiveness can come out in the form of anger, withdrawal, emotional shutdown, guilt, arguing, silence, or leaving the stressful situation. Or it might look like crying, outrage, tuning out, pouting, or performative wokeness. No matter how it emerges, it makes it hard to address racism. It ends the conversation and restores the status quo in which racism thrives.

> When disequilibrium occurs — when there is an interruption to that which is familiar and taken for granted — white fragility restores equilibrium.
>
> —Robin

Even (and sometimes especially) White people who consider themselves progressive can be defensive about racism. But their defensiveness might look different because they think they "already know this" or they "already took a class on this."

Have you ever heard a Person of Color say, "I'm so tired" when they are in a conversation about race? Often a White person who is responding predictably with white fragility triggers that fatigue in the person who is trying to help them learn and who yet again has to deal with White defensiveness. It may feel like the first time for the White person, but the thousandth time for the Person of Color. White fragility can lead quickly to one of the situations listed previously, causing the Person of Color to be left holding the problem, even though it may not have been theirs to begin with. This dynamic generates fatigue because there seems to be no way forward.

White fragility is powerful because it is backed up by historical and institutional power and control.

Examples of common triggers that can activate white fragility:

- Suggesting that a White person's viewpoint comes from their White lens and might be different from that of a Person of Color
- Another White person choosing not to agree with their racial beliefs (remember the need to uphold White solidarity from Chapter 5)

- Getting feedback that their behavior has a racist impact (remember White racial innocence from Chapter 5)
- Suggesting that White people are not just individuals but also part of a racial group called White people
- Acknowledging that there are inequities among different racial groups, which challenges the myth of meritocracy
- A Person of Color talking openly about race, which challenges White taboos about doing so
- A Person of Color choosing not to protect White people's feelings and instead saying what they really think
- A Person of Color choosing not to tell their stories or answer questions about their racial experience out of self-protection
- Having a Person of Color obtain a position of power, which challenges White authority

It can be hard to know how to respond to these challenges constructively once white fragility has been activated.

I was once in a workshop with a White teacher. During one of the all-group sessions, she used the n-word when talking about one of her history classes. She spoke the entire word without abbreviating it. I always cringe when I hear that word, but even more so when a White person says it. No matter the context. I chose not to say anything, but another White colleague did, letting the group know that the word has a lot of power and that unless we talk about why it is necessary or unnecessary to use it, no one (especially a White person) should. I turned to my colleague who had spoken up and said, "Thank you," loud enough for

*everyone to hear it. The teacher threw up her hands
and said, "You all have made me feel so small. I
can't say anything anymore!" Then she walked out
of the room. —Toni[1]*

The comments that were made by Toni and her colleague
about the history teacher's choice of words initially triggered
defensiveness, or white fragility. Can you see why her reaction
foreclosed on growth or learning for herself and for the group?

First, she made it about herself. "You all have made me feel
small." To her credit, she was being honest about how she felt.
But no one forces us to feel the way we do, so she was not
taking responsibility for her reaction, and she didn't inquire
about why they said what they said, and she didn't stop to
realize that she could have made a mistake and apologized.

Second, she went to an either/or binary. "I can't say anything anymore." Because one thing she said was critiqued, she
assumed that nothing she would say could be acceptable.

Third, she left. She didn't stay to engage, to learn, even to
continue to express her hurt. The group could have talked
through the exchange with her, but she checked out.

Fourth, she lacked the skill to be able to differentiate
between her own intention and the impact of her words and
actions. Even though she did not intend to be hurtful, she had
a hurtful impact. Being accountable for one's impact is one of
the first things a person can do to defuse their own fragility, to
learn, and to repair harm.

Finally, the history teacher didn't take into consideration
the historical context of the power of the n-word to others
in the room. Perhaps to her it was just another bad word. To
Toni (and to Toni's White colleague who spoke up) it was a
word that symbolized the anti-Blackness that had put Black

people at the bottom of the racial hierarchy for hundreds of years, while putting White people at the top. The goal in speaking up was not to make the history teacher feel small, but to ensure that this tool of the racial hierarchy be treated with the sensitivity it demands so that it does not become commonplace. The n-word is not just another swear word.

Yeah, but... **isn't calling somebody "racist" just like swearing at them? If the r-word is kryptonite for White people, can't we say the n-word is kryptonite for Black people? If the n-word is off limits, shouldn't the r-word be off limits too? Why is it okay to use the term "racist" but not the n-word?**

The r-word (racist) is meant to help describe ideas, concepts, terminology, and attitudes that perpetuate racism. It is used to educate and to eliminate racism. It can freeze or immobilize White people, but that's not because it's necessarily a term used to hurt White people, but rather because White people are unpracticed at seeing things as racist. It is a term White people can get better at hearing and learning from. If White people don't want to be racist, achieving that is possible—but it will require understanding what racist attitudes and behaviors look like, unlearning them, and developing an anti-racist practice. The n-word, by contrast, has always been used to degrade and put Black people "in their place" in the racial hierarchy. The word means that Black people are inferior to all other people and that White people are superior to all other people—especially to Black people. If you don't believe in the racial hierarchy and don't want to perpetuate this false idea, you should not use the n-word. And even if you're just referring to the word—not actually using it—you need to understand its incredible power and treat it accordingly.

Yeah, but... **Black kids use the word all the time. Why can't everybody else? My friends even give me permission to use it!**

Having permission from one Black person to use the n-word does not mean that every Black person has given you permission. The history teacher clearly thought it was okay to use the word, and maybe she even used it with other Black colleagues or students with no resistance. But that does not mean it was okay with Toni. When Black people use the n-word, there's a complicated act of resistance at work in which they are reclaiming the word or taking some of the power out of it by making it their own. Many teachers and scholars would say they are still hurting themselves by doing so. Yet it's different from when non-Black people use it. We highly recommend that you look up the clip from author Ta-Nehisi Coates on "words that don't belong to everyone" to hear his thoughts about why it's different for Black people to use the n-word than it is for non-Black people to do so.[2]

The Result: White Fragility

Many surveys say that children start to develop ideas of race very early, and that White children develop a sense of White superiority as early as preschool.[3] Again, this is not usually because anybody taught them these values explicitly, but it is part of what happens when White people are socialized within a racial hierarchy like the one operating in the United States. Because many White people grew up with a sense that racism is wrong, they deny that this notion of White superiority exists. Ironically, their very moral objection to racism ends up making it hard to see how they play a role in it.

Dr. Ruth Frankenberg was a White lesbian writer and anthropologist of Jewish descent who was a pioneer in the field of Whiteness studies. She was one of the first White people to write about the invisible and significant impact of Whiteness.[4] Her interviews with White women for the book *White Women, Race Matters* explain White patterns of understanding racism in a way that laid the foundation for understanding white fragility today.

A common pattern displayed by White people who don't want to be racist involves protecting one's moral reputation in the form of defensiveness, rather than recognizing or changing their participation in systems of inequity. A typical reaction is to explain away racist results by offering a perfectly logical explanation (PLE) for why a given situation turned out the way it did. A PLE is defined as "a way to explain away any examples of racism a Person of Color provides by focusing on individual incidents and not seeing patterns of repeated behaviors or situations."[5] Here is an example of a PLE:

The Gay Straight Alliance (GSA) only has White students. When club members are asked why there are no Kids of Color, the PLE sounds like this: *There are no gay Kids of Color. If they came to our meetings, they'd be totally welcome.* The kids in the GSA may not know the gay, lesbian, bi, trans, and gender-nonconforming Kids of Color. But they are present—in every school. The PLE explains away the phenomenon without addressing possible reasons for it—or taking responsibility for it where appropriate. The Whiteness of the GSA (and the racial belonging that its members feel) may be invisible to the students in the club. Because of the social segregation of the school, and the variety of issues faced by queer kids of different racial backgrounds, the GSA actually might not feel like a safe and welcoming place for Kids of Color. Rather than explain a phenomenon away with a PLE, the more productive response would be to say, "Huh. I don't know. Why *aren't* there more Kids of Color in the GSA?" After exploring this question, GSA members can begin to shift how they do things to make the club be a place where everyone belongs.

Because white fragility often leads to denial of racism, it ends up being White people themselves who set the standard for what is considered racist. Having very little practice or understanding about racism, White people might say, "I was not being racist," or "That comment was not racist," thereby becoming the judge of what is or is not racist, even though they are uninformed and are not the victims.

When challenged on race, White people often claim that *they* are the ones being victimized, attacked, or bullied. When they are seen as victims, they can deny the benefits of being White. This often means that they become the focus of attention, and sometimes a Person of Color ends up taking care of them.

> *While out with friends, I was snubbed by our White waiter. He asked everyone else how they were doing several times and hardly gave me eye contact, even when I was placing my order. I was the only Person of Color at the table. One of my White friends noticed. She apologized to me for his behavior and started to cry. I ended up rubbing her back and letting her know that I was okay. As I step back now, I question who was the victim there? And who was taking care of whom? —Toni*

White people often claim the language of abuse when being self-defensive. Words like "trauma," "attack," or "bullying" play into the narrative that People of Color (particularly Black people) are dangerous and violent. Consider the following story in which Ali perceived feedback as an "attack."

> *An Indian American colleague told me that something I had done was racist. I was trying to better understand it by discussing it with a White colleague, and I said, "She attacked me." My White colleague said, "Did she really attack you? Did it get physical?" I said, "No, she just told me that what I did was wrong." My White colleague said, "But why did you use the word 'attack'? Was she loud? Did she swear?" As I looked back at the conversation, I realized that nothing from that interaction could be called an attack. It was just a very tame conversation at a reception, over crackers and cheese, during which she gave me honest feedback about my choices—feedback that I, in fact, had requested. I realized that it felt like an attack because she had described an impact that was so different from my intent. The interaction left me feeling humiliated, exposed, vulnerable—not because of what she did or how she talked to me, but because of how it made me see my own behavior through her lens, and see how my choices had had a negative effect. It was my white fragility that perceived her straightforward points as an attack. —Ali*

The tendency to describe an event based on how it makes one feel—rather than on the objective behavior of the other party—is common. White people often say they felt "attacked" when talking about receiving feedback. One of the reasons it's important to differentiate between *feeling* attacked and *being* attacked is that the word "attack" or "violence" plays into common stereotypes about People of

Color. False accusations of attack not only perpetuate these stereotypes but can be dangerous to People of Color who are trying to speak their truth or help White people learn.

White people don't have enough practice dealing with racial stress, so they often want it to stop as soon as possible. A more racially just society would require that White people build the skills and capacity to engage racial stress without checking out, shutting down, or walking away. As it is now, according to sociologist Eduardo Bonilla-Silva, "Many white people are not equipped to explore their racial perspectives in order to shift their understanding of racism."[6]

These issues are important not just because of how people *look* in the classroom, workplace, or social setting. White fragility may appear as defensiveness, whining, and other undesirable behaviors that make operating in these settings harder for everyone. But when you add together all the white fragility of all the White people in the US, the sum is what Robin calls the "sociology of dominance." It functions together as a "means to protect, maintain, and reproduce white supremacy." Whether that's the intention or not, it is the result.

But it doesn't have to be that way. White people can get better. As one person in a workshop Robin led said, "It would be revolutionary" if People of Color "could give White people feedback, and if White people could receive it graciously, reflect, and work to change the behavior." If White people could minimize their fragility, if they could build "muscle" and flexibility to increase their range of motion in discussing matters of race, if they could take feedback and learn from it—the results would literally be revolutionary. But this cannot be achieved if White people stay stuck in the idea that racism is only perpetrated by intentionally mean people.

A Black workshop participant once told me it would be revolutionary

if white people could simply receive our feedback,

reflect, and work to change their behavior.

Afterthoughts

Journal

What are some concrete ways to challenge defensiveness in yourself and others?

DISCUSSION

Explain the triggers listed in this chapter in your own words, and share examples of each in daily life.

Chapter 8

WHAT DOES WHITE FRAGILITY LOOK LIKE IN ACTION AND HOW DOES IT GET IN THE WAY?

Feelings that underlie white fragility lead to behaviors that are then justified by defensive statements that are thought or said.

FEELINGS ⟶ BEHAVIORS ⟶ JUSTIFICATIONS

This trajectory in turn leads to placing blame on People of Color for not delivering feedback correctly. White fragility sets the terms of engagement.

The phrase "white fragility" sounds like weakness. It sounds like if you tap a fragile person on the shoulder, they will collapse into a pile of shards and dust. But the thing about fragility is that it rarely gets that far. Because the fragile person defends against such contact so vigorously, they might never have their shoulder tapped. Fragility actually becomes an incredibly durable wall of resistance that prevents feedback, communication, sharing, connection. Why, though? What are people protecting against?

White fragility is rooted in feelings, feelings that come up when people are asked to think and talk about race or racism. As we have said, these conversations can be uncomfortable. But despite the discomfort, White people are generally able to talk about racism and white supremacy in the abstract. The real defensiveness starts when it gets personal. If you are White, think back to race conversations in which you felt upset or confused. Perhaps you can remember a time when someone told you that something you did or said hurt them, or that it had a racist impact.

1. What were the feelings you experienced?
2. How did you behave as a result of those feelings?

If you are a Person of Color, consider a time when a conversation you had about race upset or confused the White person you were talking to.

1. What did they do?
2. How did that response make you feel?
3. How did you behave as a result of those feelings?

Pause. Take a minute to really think about these questions. It might be good to use your journal here.

One of the most common feelings that White people experience in these circumstances is fear. It might be fear of offending, fear of saying the wrong thing, fear of looking stupid. It might also be the fear of being misunderstood or of not knowing what to say. It's a fear of having good intentions that have a bad impact. It's a fear of social rejection. The feelings people report include the following:

FEELINGS

SCARED   ATTACKED   ANGRY

GUILTY   SINGLED OUT   SHAME

ACCUSED   OUTRAGED   INSULTED

JUDGED   SILENCED

Do any of these sound familiar? They are common feelings that come up for White people when they find themselves face to face with racism, especially their own. The feelings lead to certain behaviors, most of which are meant to protect against feeling the feels. These behaviors are, by and large, defensive. They include:

BEHAVIORS

So . . . what is wrong with having feelings and then acting on them? Good question. The problem with the well-worn pattern of *feeling attacked and then crying* or *feeling accused*

and then withdrawing or *feeling guilty and then arguing* is that it becomes a barrier to connection. If a White person is trying to better understand racism, to avoid causing hurt, to stop treating people differently based on their race, then having defensive feelings and acting on them means that they are going to end up farther away from their goal. These behaviors will actually make it harder to learn from People of Color, to hear their honest experiences, to stay in connection, to make change.

Here's what often happens: A Person of Color experiences racism and resolves to talk about it. When they bring it up, the White person begins to feel all those feelings, rooted in fear. They throw up their hands, they cry, they argue, they deny their contribution to what happened. Then the Person of Color is silenced, sometimes even punished for making White people feel bad. This shuts down the conversation and stops the flow of understanding.

> *After a particularly difficult moment in a workshop that I was attending, a White woman approached me to apologize for something she had said. I thanked her for the apology. She continued apologizing and started to cry. Then she said, "As a woman, I can understand how that statement could have been hurtful." I thanked her several times more. I guess she was waiting for me to accept her apology, to let her know it was okay. But it wasn't okay, and I wasn't ready to accept her apology. When I told her that, she didn't speak to me again for the remainder of the workshop. —Toni*

I have a story similar to Toni's in which I was the White person who stopped talking. I did something offensive in the first year of my graduate program. It was orientation week, and I didn't know anybody yet. I asked a Colleague of Color to give me feedback on what I had done. She told me that I was correct in my suspicion that it was offensive, and she said I shouldn't have done it. She was direct and honest, but she wasn't unkind. I was so ashamed of myself that I didn't talk to that classmate for the next two years! —Ali

Shame can have a deep effect on people. You can see from the examples above that both Ali and the White person Toni was talking to did not know how to proceed from their mistakes. And you can also see that Toni was hurt and was not prepared to offer forgiveness, even though she repeatedly thanked her colleague for the apology. This is where we get stuck. When the going gets tough, White people often duck out of the conversation, dodge the suggestion that they did something wrong, try to explain it away, or fight back. It's similar to the fight, flight, freeze reaction that people have to things they fear. In uncomfortable racial interactions, White people do one of those three things because they are afraid or ashamed. In both Toni's and Ali's stories, the White person had a "flight" response.

But can you see how the connection gets blocked by the defense? Rather than connect, listen, and learn, the person's defenses go up. Once someone's defenses are up, it's very hard to continue to communicate about what happened. That's when the justifications begin.

People's defenses sound different depending on who they are. I can sense that I'm starting to get defensive when I hear a little voice in my head saying, "Do you know how many books I've read on this subject?! Do you even know that I write books about race?" It's as if I think people will see me as less racist if they know that I write books about race. In reality, it's the opposite: they will see me as less racist if I listen to how I hurt them, if I discover more about my unintended impact, if I admit my racism and ask to learn more about it. If I just tell them how many books I've read or written, they'll think I'm an arrogant jerk who doesn't know how to take feedback. Whenever I hear that little voice in my head talking about how much I've read and written, I say to myself, "You are getting defensive about something. What is it you don't want to hear?" It's a sign to listen more closely to the person in front of me. —Ali

Other defensive whispers/justifications that might pop up in people's heads—and sometimes pop out of their mouths—include:

The desire to avoid being held responsible for a racist impact is strong. After a person gets defensive, they rely on particular mainstream assumptions to explain why they shouldn't have to listen, change, or learn.

Here are some of the assumptions. We will try to explain the problem with each one by one:

Assumptions

- **Racism is simply personal prejudice.** The difference between racism and personal prejudice is that racism is backed up by a system.
- **I am free of racism.** Racial bias is not a good thing, but it is a common thing. It's not likely that any White person is free of racism. But they can get closer to free if they stay open and willing to learn.
- **I will be the judge of whether racism has occurred.** White people don't always see how People of Color are treated, what they experience, or how years of accumulated mistreatment might impact their lives. White people are often unpracticed at seeing racism, and therefore are not typically the best judges of whether racism has occurred.
- **Racism can only be intentional.** Intentional racism is what is called old-fashioned racism. Many people in the US have been taught to see racism as intentional and violent, like that of the KKK. But modern racism is much less overtly visible. Sometimes it's intentional; most of the time it is not. Either way it still hurts.
- **My marginalized identities (growing up poor, coming to this country as an immigrant, etc.) means that I can't be privileged.** People with marginalized identities who have faced oppression can use their own history to empathize with People of Color, who come up against a different kind of oppression. But their experiences will be a block to understanding if they presume that having one form of oppression means they understand exactly what it's like to be a Person of Color, or if they think they can't also receive racial privilege because they live with other forms of oppression.
- **I am a good person, so I can't be racist.** See the second example above.

- **I should not be made to feel uncomfortable.** Nobody is entitled to comfort 100 percent of the time, especially at the expense of someone else's comfort. Discomfort is part of learning, and it's usually a sign that growth is occurring.
- **I am feeling challenged; you are doing this wrong.** On the contrary, a person could say, "If I'm *not* feeling challenged, something must be wrong." Race conversations are challenging. Sometimes they challenge our most foundational beliefs. This is how we grow and deepen our knowledge.
- **It's unkind to point out racism.** It is only unkind to point out racism if you are invested in keeping racism alive and well. If you don't like racism and you want it to go away, it's actually kinder to point it out so that people can challenge it. It is also possible to be kind *while* pointing out racism.
- **Racists are bad individuals, so you are saying that I am a bad person.** Try to get away from the good/bad binary. Just because a person has some racial bias or racist ideas in them does not mean they are all bad. It's normal to have bias, and it's normal to have to do some introspection and learning in order to reject the racist ideas of our society. If someone tells you that you are showing racial bias, don't assume they are calling you bad—that will make it almost impossible for you to hear what they're trying to tell you. Assuming that pointing out racial bias means a person is bad will make it almost impossible to give or receive feedback.
- **If you knew me, you would know that I can't be racist.** See the example just above.
- **If I can't see it, it must not be so.** Remember that White people have a different view of the world from People of Color. White people don't necessarily see the racism that People of Color experience every day. For this reason, White people rely on hearing from People of Color in order to understand racism. If they are collectively

going to be able to understand racism and do something about it, White people have to be able to hear about the realities of People of Color.

And one more:

- **Just because you are a Person of Color doesn't mean you know more than me.** True. But if we're talking about racism, there's a good chance that the average Person of Color has had more experiences of racism, more learning about racism, more time building skills for navigating racial stress, and more practice seeing racism. So while no racial group is inherently smarter or more intelligent than another group, it is true that most People of Color—because of their life experiences—are more practiced at understanding racism, just as most women and girls are more practiced at seeing and recognizing sexism. When you swim against the current, you are aware of it in a way that people swimming with the current are not.

Stopping our racist patterns must be more important than working to convince others we don't have them. We do have them, and People of Color already know we have them; our efforts to prove otherwise are not convincing.

—Robin

The Rules of Engagement

So then what? White fragility stops individuals from connecting and learning more. Is that where it ends?

No, it's not. Because white fragility is a condition that comes from being socialized in our society, it is extremely common. White people all over the US react to feedback about their racism in similar, predictable, formulaic ways. In the same way that when we hear the news that someone has died, we usually say, "I'm so sorry to hear that," White people have a typical cultural reaction to feedback on racism. To summarize this chapter, the common reaction for White people sounds essentially like this: "No, I didn't engage in racist behavior, and I don't want to hear another word about it."

Because white fragility is so widespread, it has a systemic quality to it. By this we mean that White people across the country, in many different jobs, in many different schools, tend to react to feedback on their racism in the same defensive ways. This in turn slows the possibility of widespread change because people are defending against the very learning they need to make change.

Have you seen white fragility in action? If so, what did it look like? What impact did it have on the people who witnessed it?

Common impacts of white fragility include the following:

- maintaining White solidarity (remember this phenomenon from Chapter 5)
- preventing self-reflection
- making racism look less important or like it's "not a big deal"
- silencing the discussion
- making White people the victims
- dominating the conversation and taking it in a different direction
- taking race off the table
- protecting racial privilege
- focusing on the messenger and not the message

People of Color tend to find that their ideas and experiences around racism will not be heard unless they couch their comments *just right* so they don't trigger white fragility. Robin calls this the *rules of engagement*. It is not a published list of rules that somebody is enforcing. It's a list of behaviors that People of Color feel they must follow when talking with White people about race, because when they don't, they risk not being heard or, worse, being punished for making White people feel bad.

This is what it sounds like when white fragility has the mic, dictating the rules of engagement:

- You need to watch your tone. If you are too direct, I can't hear the feedback.
- You need to be in a close relationship with me before you can give me that kind of feedback.
- You need to give me feedback immediately. If you wait, then how important to you was it really?
- You must give me feedback privately so that you don't embarrass me.
- I need to feel "safe" while you are giving feedback ("safe" often means comfortable).
- You must release me from any responsibility for causing you harm if I say that my intentions are good.
- You need to allow me to explain myself until you can see that you just misunderstood me.

Yeah, but... **aren't some of those just effective conflict-resolution skills? It's a good idea to develop trust, or to deliver critical feedback along with some praise ... isn't it?**

Yeah. A few of the items on that list are good conflict-resolution skills. And on some days, People of Color will have the energy to use them. But even when People of Color follow all the rules of engagement, white fragility often still gets in the way of White people hearing what is being said. Beyond that, we have to remember how hard it is to offer feedback to the person who hurt or offended you. Think about the last time you delivered honest feedback. It's anxiety provoking, it's scary, it can often lead you to tears. So when People of Color deliver feedback, they are taking a big risk, and it is not easy. And it's a lot to ask that they do it *just right* in order to be heard.

Yeah, but... **if people want to be heard, why don't they say it in a way that is easier to listen to?**

This is the wrong question. The question is: Do *you* want to hear? If you are a White person who does not want to be racist, who wants to be anti-racist, then you need to hear what People of Color have to say no matter how they say it. If you truly and authentically want racial justice, then you need to be open to hearing about how you impact People of Color. If you don't want those things, maybe it doesn't matter how People of Color frame what they have to say, because you probably wouldn't hear it anyway. But if you want justice and fairness, it's important to realize the systematic ways in which White people refuse to hear from People of Color. It's very common for People of Color to put work, effort, and intention into delivering feedback juuuuuust right, and still not get heard.

The method of delivery cannot be used to delegitimize what is being illuminated or as an excuse for disengagement.

—Robin

People of Color should not be expected to hold back their truth in order to keep White people from being defensive. It's too tall an order when they have likely experienced repeated rejection of their feedback in other, similar scenarios. But if you are a White person and you are trying to offer feedback to another White person on racism, sensitive communication is of course helpful. Why is it different? It's different because White people benefit from racism, whether they are anti-racist or not. Even if another White person says something you would never say, that doesn't mean you are less implicated in a racist system than they are. It doesn't mean you know everything or can stop learning. Furthermore, other White people are more likely to learn from you if you share what you know without making it seem that you are better than they are. If you are White—because you are not the direct target of racism—take the time to deliver the feedback in a way that will support the White person in front of you to hear it. And when you see something that needs to get said, say it. The very fact that you're White means that people might hear it differently from you, especially if you call them *in* (using trust, empathy, and patience to speak to them and help them learn from their mistake) rather than call them *out* (shame them, undermine them, and make them "all bad" for making a mistake).[1]

So What Is the Response That Will Help White People Connect and Move Forward?

What if a Person of Color delivers feedback to a White person and says that the person did something racist? How can a White person respond in an anti-racist way?

1. Take the feedback as a gift.
2. Say thank you, even if it's a gift you didn't want and you don't like.
3. Take care of yourself and sort out your feelings about the gift after you are out of the presence of the person who offered it.

Fundamentally, feedback is necessary for growth. People do not offer feedback to people whom they don't want to stay in relationship with. When we accept feedback with appreciation, we show our intention, which is to stay in connection, to hear about our impact, to learn, to grow, to do better.

Say thank you. Can you imagine being offered a gift that you hand back immediately? *No, thank you. I didn't need a new watch. I don't want that book. The T-shirt you gave me is ugly.* Hopefully we would never do that! Feedback can be hard to take in sometimes, but it's also hard to offer. If someone offers you feedback, say thank you, and take the gift somewhere else to open it.

The third step is about creating the conditions for combating your own fragility. Take the gift of feedback to another anti-racist friend who can help you unpack it, and open it with them. You may not fully understand it or appreciate it. You might not want it or agree with it. Examine it with a friend or colleague who is not directly impacted by the feedback (i.e., someone outside the conflict). Try to understand it. Give it time to sink in. Learn more about it.

An antidote to white fragility is to build up own stamina to bear witness to the pain of racism that we cause, not to impose conditions that require People of Color to continually validate our denial.

—Robin

WHY NOT TEARS?

Yeah, but... **crying was listed as a defensive behavior. But why? Isn't it okay to cry?**

Of course it's okay to cry! In fact, it's important to cry. White people are often out of touch with the pain and sadness of racism. Getting emotionally in touch with that pain and sadness is part of developing a motivation to work against racism. Crying in and of itself is not bad. The behaviors discussed in this chapter are not problems on their own merits. They are problematic when they are rooted in a desire to defend oneself against hearing the truth about one's impact or about a Person of Color's experience of racism. In that context, they have a silencing effect. Or they have the effect of denying the Person of Color their feelings.

If a White person starts crying in response to feedback on their racism, the Person of Color often ends up comforting the White person. It reverses the roles. The Person of Color is in pain, but they have to comfort the person who caused them the pain. Besides crying, there are other ways that White people avoid honest discussions about the racist impact they have. These can look like anger, outrage, belligerence, even sidetracking humor. Anger, sadness, and humor are not inherently bad things to bring to a conversation, but they become destructive when they recenter the conversation around the White person's intense emotional reaction and leave out People of Color and their feelings. This is a problem when others in the

(continued)

group then accuse the Person of Color of causing difficulties, or shut down the conversation because it seems to be getting too intense. In this way, the fragility of the White people dictates what the group does, rather than the pain or needs of the People of Color.

Afterthoughts

Journal

Write about a time when you experienced your own white fragility or witnessed a White person's fragility. What did you do? How might you do things differently if you had an opportunity to do so?

Which of the defensive whispers sound familiar to you? Have you heard someone else use them? Have you said any of them? If you have said them, write about how you can counter that narrative.

DISCUSSION

With a small group, rewrite the rules of engagement from an anti-racist framework.

Chapter 9

MEDIA ANALYSIS—SOCIAL AND OTHERWISE

This chapter talks about media: the media we take in (like movies, TVs, magazines, and commercials) and the media we put out (like social media posts, comments, even texts and emails). We'll discuss how to make sure that what you post is not hurtful or racist, how to respond when others post hurtful or racist content, and then how to post anti-racist content.

First, a survey. See if you agree or disagree with the following statements:

- People have cracked jokes about my race or ethnic group online.
- People have said things that were untrue about my race or ethnic group.
- People have said rude things about me because of my race or ethnic group.

In a recent survey of Students of Color, 60 percent answered yes to "People have cracked jokes about my race or ethnic group online"; 55 percent said yes to "People have said things that were untrue about my race or ethnic group"; 36 percent said yes to "People have said rude things about me because of my race or ethnic group."[1]

Think about that. When was the last time you logged on to social media to read negative things about a group that you're a part of? If you've had that experience, recall the feelings that it brought up as you tried to figure out if you should say or do anything. Recall how it changed your experience of that social media platform. As you read through this chapter, remember that more than half of young People of Color have experienced social media as a place of marginalization and oppression. Although social media can be a space of affirmation and connection, a space of learning and enlightenment, it is also definitely a place where hurt gets perpetuated, where racism is present.

Social Media

In a survey conducted in 2020 by the Harris Poll, 83 percent of students between the ages of fourteen and nineteen said they believe that systemic racism is an issue.[2] And yet when we talked with teens for this book, many of them told us that they only discuss racism with their peers over social media. And even then they often don't post their original thoughts—they repost memes or news articles that they agree with.

There's nothing inherently wrong with repurposing content, but if a person only reposts and does not share their own thoughts, the field of opinions and ideas gets significantly narrowed. The stakes may also then feel higher to people who are afraid to say what they think if it's different from the post, because they know everyone is standing by, ready to critique whatever gets posted. We end up having a society of critics and very few original thinkers.

What we heard from our focus groups in preparation for this book is that many White students are afraid of saying the wrong thing when it comes to race. White students seemed to want to say something but felt afraid of offending or taking up too much space. Ironically, Students of Color recognized this fear in their White classmates and said they wished those classmates would take more risks, ask more questions, say what they think, speak up.

White students said, "We don't know the right thing to say." Their Peers of Color said, "We want to hear from them anyway." Talking things through—even when one's ideas are imperfect or undeveloped—is one of the only ways to keep learning. When White people stay silent, it conveys the idea (intentionally or unintentionally) that they don't care or they don't think racism is their problem.

We suggest that one of the best ways to begin interacting is to figure out what you believe by participating in off-line conversations with others. Continue to repost responses to new stories that you are engaging in or memes that speak your mind. But when you repost, let people know with a comment why you are doing so. Explain why you are posting and what you are thinking. This is incredibly important practice for speaking up in person as well.

We heard a theme from Students of Color that it seemed as though White students often posted what they thought they were supposed to post without knowing why. Or they posted things that they hoped would make them look anti-racist. This meant that classmates posted videos of Black people dying at the hands of police. Then the Students of Color we spoke with would be lying in bed, reaching for their phone in the morning, and seeing video after video of Black pain before they even ate breakfast.

It's valuable to post such content. And it's possible that those White classmates knew that if they posted it, their more socially isolated (and racially isolated) aunt or cousin might see it—and if they didn't post it, they might not. But if you post things like this, share why you are doing so. Maybe you think it's important for people in your feed to see it. Because it might be painful for a Black classmate to see it, include a "content warning" about what people can expect. Let them know in a few short words what the post contains so that they don't click on it while just starting their day.

We suggest to White students that you use social media as a space to claim racism as a problem that you intend to deal with. Ask yourself, "How does this racist event connect to things that I have learned or been taught?" Remember that we have all been socialized in a racist system. Consider how the socialization that enabled the racist event you are posting about might show up in your own life and relationships. In your post, model self-reflection about your own learning and unlearning.

Being Anti-Racist on Social Media

Remember that on social media it's very hard to know if your repost means that you agree or disagree with a person or a meme. When you disagree with content that you're reposting, it is important to voice your disagreement. If you are commenting on someone else's post, remember that it's hard to convince anyone of anything in the comment section, particularly if they don't know you. People are most likely to take feedback from individuals they know, and to draw battle lines with individuals they don't know.

If you plan to use social media, think about how you're going to engage. When you disagree with someone's post:

- Before you write, pause. Ask yourself, "How do I actually feel about this?" Figure out your thoughts and feelings before you begin posting. Consider this a valuable moment to say what you believe.

- Disagree while expressing some part of your identity and letting people know who you are. Don't be anonymous. If your post is anonymous, respond as you would if your name were attached.
- Speak from the "I" perspective. If you are White, don't say, "My Black classmate would be offended by that." Say that *you* are offended, and explain why.
- Respond as you would if the person were standing in front of you. Don't call names, don't accuse. Be respectful to the people you are trying to connect with.
- Let the person know the impact of their post on you.
- If the person gets disrespectful, cut off the interaction. You don't have to write back, "I'm not going to engage anymore." Doing so prolongs the conflict and absorbs energy the way a black hole absorbs matter.

Some of these tips are meant to help social media be less anonymous. When everyone is hiding behind the screen and posting comments on threads with no accountability, social media becomes toxic. People don't learn. Opinions do not get cultivated or evolve; they are just pitted against each other like gladiators in an arena.

Social media has been the launching place of so many powerful campaigns, including Me Too, Black Lives Matter, and the Me and White Supremacy Workbook. Activist Layla F. Saad began a hashtag on Instagram called #MeAndWhiteSupremacy, which she used to give White people prompts that could help them learn to recognize and confront their own racism. She expanded her prompts into a downloadable workbook, which today is a *New York Times* best-selling book called *Me and White Supremacy: Combat Racism, Change the World, and Become a Good Ancestor* (and for which Robin had the honor of writing the foreword). The reason her work has resonated globally is

Layla Saad is a writer, public speaker, and host of the podcast *Good Ancestor*. She identifies as East African, Arab, British, Black, and Muslim. What started as a downloadable workbook, Saad's *Me and White Supremacy: A 28-Day Challenge to Combat Racism, Change the World, and Become a Good Ancestor*, is now a best-selling book.[3]

that she stayed engaged with people throughout the process of developing it. And beyond that, she challenged people to engage in their own ongoing process. Knowing that people would not change because of one specific post or even one powerful exchange, she invited them to begin a personal practice at home with themselves, and from there to develop the capacity to see how white supremacy impacts them.

Ambiguity of the Written Word

When you are on social media, remember that there are often multiple ways to interpret a written statement. Whether you are writing or reading, you often impose your own lens and inflection on the statement. Consider this statement:

"I didn't say she stole my purse!"

Read the sentence again and see if the meaning changes if you change which words you emphasize. How many different meanings could this sentence have?

I DIDN'T SAY SHE STOLE MY PURSE.
I DIDN'T SAY SHE STOLE MY PURSE.
I *didn't* SAY SHE STOLE MY PURSE.
I DIDN'T *say* SHE STOLE MY PURSE.
I DIDN'T SAY *she* STOLE MY PURSE.
I DIDN'T SAY SHE *stole* MY PURSE.
I DIDN'T SAY SHE STOLE *my* PURSE.
I DIDN'T SAY SHE STOLE MY *purse.*

When you write, do so in ways that leave little room for misunderstanding. When you are the reader, read what others have written in ways that leave a lot of room for possible intention.

Performative Activism

Performative activism is when people are more concerned with looking anti-racist than with being anti-racist. Performative activism can show up in a lot of different ways, but on social media it involves posting the banner of the moment without really caring very deeply about the issues or the people it impacts.

> One of my former students said that he wanted to post a blue square online to support his Jewish friends after an anti-semitic incident at his college. But he didn't want to look like he was just engaged in performative activism. I said to him, "Whether you post the blue square or not, you've answered your own question. You said you wanted to support your Jewish friends. How are you doing that? Have you reached out? Have you checked in with them? Have you let them know you're thinking about them?" Online activism is not meant to stay online. It's a way to communicate broadly, but it does not replace the importance of individual relationships. —Toni

After George Floyd was murdered, one of my friends wrote online, "Everyone says Black Lives Matter, but no one has called to see if I'm okay." When I first read her post, I felt indignant. I thought, "You know I care about you! Am I supposed to reach out to all of my Black friends to let them know I care about them?!" After a few minutes of reflection, I realized that was exactly what I needed to do. If I really believe Black lives matter, if I really care about the pain my Black friends were potentially experiencing in that moment, I needed to call them and let them know I care. Not to perform wokeness, but to connect across the trauma and sadness. I also needed to be open to giving them space if they indicated they wanted it. —Ali

Another way that performative activism sneaks into people's social media feeds is when White people tell stories about themselves or post pictures of themselves as White saviors—for example, by posting a photo of themselves traveling to an African country and being surrounded by African children. Performative activism centers the person (in this case the White person) rather than the need, the people they are working with, or the systems that cause the need.

What are the alternatives to performative activism? They include:

- **Inquiry**—Trying to learn more. Being honest about what you don't know.
- **Solidarity**—Finding out what people want and need, and bringing attention to those things.

- **Authentic relationships**—Building relationships that go beyond one vacation or one photograph.

What to Do About Fake News

Social media has been widely critiqued for furthering social divides in the US and across the globe. It amplifies one's own point of view, feeding people news stories and memes that they already agree with, while eliminating those they don't. There are many fake-news sites—both liberal and conservative—that rile people up on social media by putting out stories of events that never happened, or that happened years ago. Part of effective anti-racist action means being responsible about what you repost. There is enough injustice in the world that we need to work against—we don't need to get stirred up over things that never actually occurred. Reposting such stories also makes our arguments (and our feeds) less credible.

In addition to ensuring that you are getting your news from actual news sources, beware of the fake news you may see posted on friends' accounts. How can you tell if a news article is fake? Cindy Otis, a former CIA analyst, wrote a book on identifying fake news. If you are tempted to repost an article, but you're not sure that it's legitimate, here are a few of her tips:[4]

1. Check the URL.
2. Check the date.
3. Investigate the source.
4. Watch out for spelling mistakes and poor grammar.
5. See if other news outlets are reporting the story.

6. Identify who is telling the story and why.
7. Look at where the author gets their information.
8. Ask yourself if there is more to the story.
9. Go to fact-checking websites such as Snopes.com.

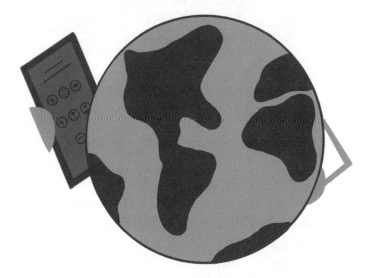

Otis compares social media to a global game of telephone. One unthinking tweet can go out that isn't necessarily true, and it can blow up into a worldwide news phenomenon in a matter of hours. To be sure that you are not spreading fake news, Otis recommends the following:[5]

1. Figure out what kind of post and account you are looking at. Is it an advertisement? A comment from a friend? An official news source? A quote?
2. Find the real experts. Are the people that you're following people who studied, teach, or work in that field?
3. Don't be fooled by the number of likes, shares, and comments on a social media post.

4. Learn how to spot fake accounts created by bots that have generic profiles or little information on their profiles.
5. Watch out for political memes.
6. Don't share things you already know are not true.
7. Share good sources of news and information.
8. Don't feed the trolls.
9. Flag fake news.

If you only get your news from social media, challenge yourself to find more news outlets, whose reporters abide by a code of journalistic ethics. Most importantly, don't get all your news from just one source.

Dangers and Benefits of Social Media

One of the dangers of social media is that you get pulled into echo chambers where everyone is saying the same thing. You don't even need to know how to explain what you believe— because everyone agrees.

The benefit of social media is that it offers a way to get your message out to a lot of people. For example, two sisters decided to leave the Westboro Baptist Church because of the conversations they had with another user on Twitter. As members of Westboro while growing up, they were expected to participate in campaigns throughout the United States opposing what they believed to be the country's supposedly sinful "gay agenda." They even protested in front of funerals of fallen soldiers because they thought that the nation deserved to lose people in battle due to that perceived agenda. Following the rise of social media, the church used it as a platform for more campaigning. In the process, the sisters began an ongoing conversation with a Jewish man who followed their accounts. He was able to poke holes in the arguments they had been taught their entire lives. He was successful because he built a relationship with them over time. Social media gives us an extraordinary opportunity to be in relationship with people whom we might never meet otherwise. It gives us a chance to see outside our boxes. It has an amazing power—and we need to figure out how we use that power for good.

A few years ago, a congressperson got voted out of office in Alabama because he was a known pedophile. As I understood it, it was Black women's votes that really gave him the final push. When I saw that he had lost his race, I wrote on my Facebook page, "Way to go, Black women!" A White friend, who is really more of a distant acquaintance from the town where I grew up, responded, "If I wrote, 'Way to go, White women,' would that be racist?" I considered her question. It is different to cheer on White people as a group than it is to cheer on Black people as a group. I wrote back to her, "Yes, but I'm not going to go into that right now. If you want to talk more, let's talk in person." She unfriended me. As soon as I said, "Yes," it shut the conversation down. She doesn't know my definition of racism. My guess is that she hasn't read much about race and racism. If I hadn't stepped outside the zip code where I grew up, I might have said the same thing. I shut the discussion down by doing what I thought was right in the moment, but in retrospect I would have liked to have had a conversation with her. If

> *I had a chance for a do-over, I would've written,*
> *"This is way more complicated than a yes or no*
> *answer," and then I would have asked her to chat by*
> *phone. —Toni*

Yeah, but… **Toni's story makes it sound like you can't cheer for White people as a group. Why can't you, if you can cheer for other racial groups?**

The thing about Whiteness as a group identity is that it was created for the sake of preserving benefits for White people. It makes sense to cheer on members of your racial group if you are Black or Asian American or Latinx or Native, because you are cheering for people who were given inferior resources, rights, and opportunities—and told to compete against people with significant advantages. Being anti-racist and cheering for the White team are antithetical—they don't go together. We can—and should—cheer for White people when they use their individual and collective power to face isms. So why can't we cheer for White people just because they're White?

See if this example helps. Say a Deaf figure-skating team wins a competition. You could imagine other Deaf people cheering for that team, specifically because they are Deaf and because they relate to some of the challenges they have faced as Deaf people. Now imagine some hearing people see this and say, "That's ableist! If I can't cheer for hearing people as a group, you shouldn't be cheering for Deaf people as a group." But why would hearing people cheer for other hearing people simply based on the fact that they are members of the same mainstream group? It's different when you are part of a group that has faced ongoing, collective marginalization.

Yeah, but… **that sucks.**

We get that. Remember that the end goal is not for everyone to have one month to celebrate their history or one day a year to hold a parade for their identity group. The end goal is for every human being on every day of every year to be respected for the fullness of who they are. The end goal is for all of us to know one another's histories and how they impact our present. The end goal is for each of us to be safe, affirmed, accepted, and celebrated, exactly how we are.

You have no doubt heard someone respond to the statement "Black Lives Matter" with "All Lives Matter" or even the question "Don't all lives matter?" And of course all lives *should* matter, but we don't currently live in a world in which they do. So we have to identify those whose lives haven't traditionally mattered so that we can create that better world.

Costumes and Jokes

Many of the issues we have seen on social media stem from people making jokes, reposting jokes, or posting pictures of themselves wearing costumes that are deeply offensive. This section will hopefully support you in being discerning about issues to consider with regard to costumes and humor.

> *At a university where I worked many years ago, the sororities and fraternities decided to develop an anti-racist training for all their members. This was after a Greek-sponsored Cinco de Mayo party in which mostly White people (although not exclusively White people) dressed up in deeply offensive, stereotypical ways. When other students on campus saw postings from the party on social media, they took*

offense. Many of the partygoers felt deeply ashamed.
The university was embarrassed, too. The sororities
and fraternities were fined and punished. But more
importantly, the students felt embarrassed that they
hadn't known better. This event led to extensive
training that was based on the idea that an educated
person needs racial competency skills to contribute
to a healthy multiracial community and society. The
students' lack of racial competency damaged their
peers and their community. The training was enacted
to help them gain the skills they needed to right their
wrongs but also to do better as they went out into
the world. —Ali

How does a person make sure to draw the line between a
fun party idea and an offensive one? Between a funny joke
and a racist one? How do you decide whether a costume
is culturally appropriative or honoring? These issues don't
have easy solutions. Some schools use a list of questions for
students to answer for themselves when considering costumes
or jokes:

- Is my costume/joke supposed to be funny? Is the humor
  based on making fun of real people—of human traits or
  cultures?
- Does my costume/joke reduce cultural differences to
  gags or stereotypes?
- Does my costume/joke perpetuate stereotypes, misinformation, or historical and cultural inaccuracies?
- Would I be embarrassed or ashamed if someone from
  the group I'm portraying saw me wearing this costume/
  telling this joke?

These four questions can go a long way in helping you think about the ways in which humor or costumes will have a negative impact on the People of Color who see you, hear your joke, or glance at your picture on their feed.

Media Analysis

The last thing we need to talk about when it comes to media is all the media we consume. From a young age, we take in *Dora the Explorer*, "Conjunction Junction," Disney, Pixar, Pokémon, gaming, commercials, Legos, American Girl dolls, Minecraft, Harry Potter, Percy Jackson, *The Hunger Games*, *The Lord of the Rings*, Hollywood movies like *Moana* and *Frozen*, TV shows like *American Idol*, YouTube videos, *Nailed It!*, and so much more. We consume hours of input every day. Having strong media-analysis skills can help you be thoughtful about what images and subtle messages are going into your head. For an example relating to sexism, the blockbuster movie *Frozen* is the story of two sisters, but the males in the movie speak 59 percent of the time![6]

Again, one useful metric to use as you analyze media is this: Does this show or game maintain a racial hierarchy? Are the White people portrayed as smarter, more capable, more worthy of unification with their families in the end? Are the People of Color silly, violent, laughable, objectified, overly sexualized? Is the cast completely White?

With each show you analyze, you may feel like some of these things are true, but not all the time or in every episode. Consider, then, the media that you take in over the course of one week or one month. How many episodes have White protagonists? Do the Characters of Color have storylines? Names? Are characters depicted in one-dimensional, stereo-typical ways?

Frederick Gooding Jr. has written up a set of archetypes that often appear in mainstream media depicting People of Color, as well as prototypes that are common when depicting White people.[7] Being familiar with these archetypes and prototypes can help us have a more nuanced understanding of media, including but not limited to commonly portrayed stereotypes.

People of Color Archetypes[8]

1. Angel Figure
2. Background Figure
3. Comic Relief
4. Menace to Society
5. Physical Wonder
6. Utopic Reversal

1. Angel Figure
- Provides assistance or emotional catharsis to the central White character.
- Is virtually devoid of any external relationships outside of those with the White character(s).
- White protagonist solicits angel figure for advice/assistance.
- In spite of their wisdom and insight, they are more limited in scope than the White protagonists they assist.

2. Background Figure
- Little to no dialogue.
- Minimal screen time.
- Little to no bearing on plot development.
- Moviegoers may see background figures as a reflection of a diversifying film industry, but they are a low-risk, low-cost investment in "visual diversity."

3. Comic Relief

- Ethnicity/culture serves as fodder for humor.
- Person of Color's culture-specific traits and/or characteristics are contrasted against "normal" White behavior.
- Person of Color's conduct is marked by exaggerated facial expressions, voice intonations, and physical gestures.

4. Menace to Society

- Minority characters in urban dramas, cop, or drug-themed movies.
- Typically portrayed by Males of Color.
- Physically imposing presence, sometimes partially clothed.
- Character is purveyor of unorganized, aggressive, or "random" violence.
- Character of Color contrasted against more "civil" White protagonists.
- Often involves the use of rappers and/or hip-hop artists.

5. Physical Wonder

- Primarily valued for physical prowess.
- Explicit acknowledgement of physical stature, talent, or skill set.
- Often overly sexualized, often bare-chested, scantily clad, or nude.

6. Utopic Reversal

- Occupies a high-ranking position, usually in isolation from other People of Color.
- Authority or power is not fully exercised or recognized onscreen.

- Rarely depicted in informal, personal, or romantic settings.

White Archetypes

1. Assumed Affluent
2. Family Tied
3. Hero
4. Intellectual
5. The Manipulator
6. The Romantic

1. Assumed Affluent
- Seldom seen working or thinking about money.
- Plenty of money at his/her disposal.
- Upper middle class, portrayed as "average."

2. Family Tied
- White characters are the universal default.
- White family unit serves as emotional anchor of movie or show.
- Stresses the strength and value of relationships among White family members.
- Reunification/preservation of core family unit is persistent goal of story line.

3. The Hero
- The hero is almost always a White male.
- The "destined one" or "chosen one" or "lucky one" or "smart one."
- Authorized to do whatever is necessary to complete his objective (which typically includes saving the world).

4. The Intellectual

- White character who is inherently knowledgeable about anything and everything.
- Omniscience is often displayed—can fight, build houses, catch criminals, fly planes.
- Audiences are trained to look to White characters to provide information essential to the plot.

5. The Manipulator

- Displays a strong sense of entitlement.
- The lone, morally empowered citizen does not live by the rules and often must break them in order to succeed.
- Rejects their circumstances at face value and changes them to fit their needs.
- White characters frequently move from a position where they lack control to the point where they become the primary person in control.

6. The Romantic

- Romance between two White (heterosexual) protagonists central to the plot.
- The protagonist often "gets the girl" at the end.
- Frequently involves an "average" White male character paired with a stereotypically attractive female character.

Yeah, but... **now I know what the archetypes, prototypes, and stereotypes are. What do I do? Stop watching these shows? Stop laughing at them?**

This is a personal decision. You may decide to stop watching certain shows. You may no longer appreciate humor that subtly reinforces a hierarchy you don't believe in. You may decide to start calling it as you see it, pointing it out verbally to whoever you're watching with or making note of it later to a friend. You may note it mentally but keep enjoying the show. The point is not to stop consuming media altogether, but to have some control over what goes into your head—or *how* it goes into your head. The goal is to be mindful of the jokes, stereotypes, archetypes, and prototypes in the media you consume so that you don't mindlessly spit them back out or let them take up permanent residence in your brain without your consent.

You are likely part of a generation that has been connected to smart phones and social media from before you could talk. This has had a huge impact on how you see and interact with the world. The key to having strong racial-analysis skills is taking time off-line, including as you read this book, to figure out what you believe. That way, when you are online, you can show up authentically.

In the next chapter, we will talk about taking action—moving from fragility to agility.

Afterthoughts

ACTIVITY

Design your own meme based on something that you have learned from this book about anti-racism.

Chapter 10

FROM FRAGILITY TO AGILITY

Dear Readers of Color:

I hope that as you have read the pages of this book you have felt affirmed and supported. As a person who identifies as Black, I understand the unique struggles we face as we walk the wrong way on the moving sidewalk. I am grateful for the partnerships I have formed with White people who are walking with me. I hope you have a multiracial array of people in your life helping you to dismantle systems, like I do.

Up to this point, we have been careful to make sure that we are writing to a multiracial audience. In this last chapter, we don't. It is a set of instructions for White people specifically to move beyond their fragility into a place of action. There are a few ways that you can read this chapter as a Person of Color. Read it with your White friends in mind. What are some ideas that you can bring to your conversations with them? Or read it with your own dominant identities in mind. Where do you experience fragility, and how might these ideas help you? Read it with your ancestors in mind. We stand on the shoulders of people who have laid a path for us. My commitment is to them. How can I learn all I am able to and do all I can to honor their legacy—continuing the fight toward equity and justice?

With respect, Toni

You've made it this far in the book, which means that you know what white fragility is, where it comes from, what it looks like, what it sounds like, the damage it wreaks, and some of the systemic causes that make it so widespread. In this final chapter, we want to discuss what to do about it and, more importantly, how you can challenge your own white fragility and work against racism. We call this chapter "From Fragility to Agility"[1] because we want you to feel able, agile, and competent as you consider how to move forward. As you move away from fragility and move toward action, we want you to expand your range of motion so that you can navigate racial stressors and approach racism in ways that are strategic, that play to your strengths, and that ultimately lead to a more just world.

This chapter is divided into three parts—self, others, and your sphere of influence—all of which are connected to building your agility for taking action.

Self

As you think about taking action, remember that for White people, self-reflection is the first step. If you are White, white fragility will always be a potential part of your life. Just like bias, it's likely to keep cropping up, even when you've noticed it and tried to stop letting it control your actions. So stay engaged in learning, growing, and taking feedback. Don't be discouraged by the missteps. Be reassured that just as building muscle produces micro tears in the muscle fibers, building racial competence will involve moments when you face your own imperfections, wrong assumptions, and mismatched intent and impact. This is normal. It becomes a problem when you stop taking in the feedback, when you refuse to self-reflect.

An idea in macroeconomics called anti-fragility[2] can be useful to understanding how a person can grow out of white fragility. Anti-fragility is not the absence of mistakes or the presence of perfection. It is the idea that growth happens *because of* mistakes and stress. Encountering racial stress, by that logic, does not weaken us—it makes us more capable. Anti-fragility suggests that stress, conflict, mistakes, and feedback can make a person stronger.

Anti-fragility will require deep humility to recover from mistakes, to show up in all your imperfections, to shift your lens as you have started to do in the process of reading this book. But when you do these things, you increase the possibility for authentic connection and growth.

> *A Mexican American student recently told me that his college was conducting anti-racism trainings for students and faculty after a number of racist incidents had occurred. He said he was happy the school was taking measures to help people learn, but the trainings seemed to make White people "act weird." He said his peers no longer used his name, for fear of calling him the wrong name and committing a microaggression. He said someone asked him where he was from, and the other person they were with smacked them and said, "We're not supposed to ask that. It's a microaggression." The two just walked off, leaving him standing there. He said, "Please help people learn, but tell them not to get weird. I still want to connect." —Ali*

Remember that making mistakes is one of the risks we take by being human. This student's White classmates were so afraid of being wrong or offensive that they simply disconnected. This gets us nowhere. "Acting weird," as this student put it, is not better than making mistakes. Part of developing agility is knowing that you will make mistakes. As long as you are willing to make amends and learn, your mistakes will actually make you stronger and more racially competent. This is the practice of anti-fragility. This is how you move from fragility to agility.

Remember That Competence
Requires Practice

> I met a high school junior who told me that she
> once asked some White classmates to stop using
> the n-word. They said, "What do you care? You're
> White!" She said, "Yeah, I'm White. And that
> word dehumanizes people. And I get offended by
> dehumanization. So I'm offended. Please stop using
> that word." —Ali

Learning how to navigate racially stressful situations, like
speaking up in the way that the young woman in this story
did, takes practice. It's not something you can do just because
you decide you want to, or because you believe it's right.
Think how many times an athlete has to repeat a given
motion in practice so they can get it right during competition. Think how many strokes an artist must take before
they know how to lay down a few well-placed lines to render
a portrait. Knowing what to say or how to say it—or even
being able to recognize racism—takes practice. Every time
you do so, that is practice. You may not get it perfect, you
may not love what you said or how you said it, but just
remind yourself that you are practicing anti-fragility and
helping others to do the same. It can also be helpful to have
a group in which you practice recognizing and intervening in
racism.

When someone does or says something racist in your presence, it can feel like an out-of-body experience—like you're
watching yourself respond (or not respond) from far away.
Often we think of the perfect response about twenty minutes

later, when our heart rate slows to normal and our brain comes back online. For this reason, psychologist Howard Stevenson suggests that people take a few steps before they speak up in a racially stressful moment:[3]

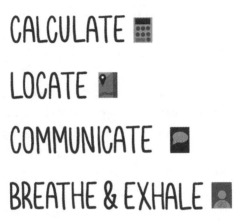

CALCULATE

LOCATE

COMMUNICATE

BREATHE & EXHALE

Calculate the degree of stress you are experiencing on a scale of one to ten.

Locate the places in your body where you are experiencing that stress.

Communicate with yourself about the self-talk you are engaging in as a result of the stress. How are you interpreting what is happening?

Breathe in.

Exhale.

This process helps you ground yourself so that you don't leave your body, and after doing it you will be more ready to respond to any stressful situation—racial or otherwise. It may seem that it will take a lot of time, but again, with practice it becomes something you can do in a matter of seconds. Practicing this process and practicing responding are both ways that will help you be better able to react.

Stay in Relationship

Stay in relationship with People of Color. It's very hard for a White person to know how to take action against racism if they do not have honest and authentic relationships with People of Color. That does not mean you should rely on People of Color to educate you about racism or tell you how to take action. And it doesn't mean you should try to befriend someone just because they are a Person of Color. But look for points of connection with the people who are already part of your life. Consider putting more time into relationships that already exist. It's possible that an unconscious belief in your separateness or differentness may be preventing a relationship from growing. It's possible that an unconscious belief in the racial hierarchy may have meant you made unfair or unwarranted judgements. Look at what might be standing in the way of building relationships, and take a step toward reaching out.

> *Early in my anti-racism journey, I had an unconscious belief that only Black people were real People of Color. I knew that Asian Americans and Latinx people were technically People of Color, but I minimized their experiences of racism and disregarded their voices. At that time I didn't really know any people who were Native, so their experiences were not visible to me. I also felt that if a Black person wasn't particularly radical, then their experiences didn't count. I spent a lot of time judging the authenticity of People of Color rather than building relationships and learning from the many different experiences of the people around me.*

When I opened myself up to authentic relationships with people of all racial backgrounds, I found that I became more knowledgeable about racism and how it impacts others. But even more importantly, I found that I became more invested in undoing racism, both in my society and in myself. Suddenly I found that this wasn't about an abstract system of racism that existed in a theoretical world. People I loved were dehumanized by this system. Nothing could be more motivating. —Ali

Do It for Yourself, Not for the Praise

In my early days of teaching I was constantly going into my boss's office to tell her about the neat and cool thing that I was doing with my students. I would like to think it was just about sharing, but it really was about validation. I wanted her to say, "Toni, you are doing a good job." Because she wanted me to have a bit more confidence in myself and to celebrate my own wins without needing her validation, she bought me one of those tiny hand-clappers. That way I could cheer myself on. —Toni

Have you ever seen someone who seems to want everyone to know how "woke" or aware of anti-racism they are? This type of performance is problematic in that it once again takes the focus away from People of Color and puts it on White people, in this case demanding that White people be affirmed for acknowledging something that, for many people in the world, is not new.

This doesn't mean you shouldn't take action or you should hide whatever action you do take. If you feel yourself in deep need of affirmation for what you are doing, find a trusted friend or colleague whom you can talk to about that need. Remember Toni's hand-clapping story. Find a way that you can affirm yourself, or find affirmation in one trusted friendship, so that you can meet your need without demanding that everybody in your world applaud you. It also doesn't mean that what you have done is unimportant. It's just that White people often get credit for confronting racism, while People of Color often get punished. And when People of Color are dealing with racism every day without getting credit, it can be hard to be asked to applaud people who are just starting to see it.

In addition, be sure that you are listening—really listening—to the stories, realities, and requests from Friends, Peers, and Colleagues of Color. Remember that you cannot fully understand how racism operates in your sphere of influence without hearing how the People of Color around you are impacted. You cannot change the fact that your lens is White. But you can compensate for that fact by making sure it's not the only lens you use for seeing and understanding your world. Listening deeply to People of Color is one way to do this.

Yeah, but… **does this mean that from now on, People of Color should always speak before White people speak, and anything that makes a Person of Color less central is wrong?**

Not necessarily. In a racially just world, White people and People of Color share the stage, pass the mic, work together, learn from each other. In a racially just world, no person's voice gets more airtime or more value because of their race. It may be hard to see if you are someone whose voice is generally valued, but within a racial hierarchy White people are often listened to more than People of Color. White voices are often given more credibility, and White people are often granted more space to share. So dismantling a racial hierarchy means balancing that out and making sure that time is shared. When it comes to dismantling racism, if a White person is draining the energy of People of Color by acting in ways that are about themselves and their own feelings, then they're not helping dismantle racism. It's not that White people don't matter. But if you're trying to dismantle racism, putting the emotions and experiences of People of Color back in second place (below those of White people on the racial hierarchy) doesn't change things. So, again, it's not that White people's feelings and ideas are not important, but they are not *more* important or *less* important than those of a Person of Color. In terms of undoing racism, hearing and understanding the experiences and feelings of People of Color is what helps us change things. That's why fragility is a blocker. It blocks the hearing, it blocks the understanding, it blocks the road to change.

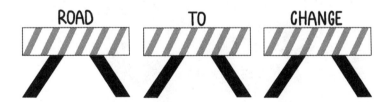

Find White Anti-Racist Role Models

Dr. Beverly Daniel Tatum says that White people need role models. When White people look around to see how to be White in our society, they often see only three possible options: colorblind, ignorant, or racist.[4] There are plenty of

Howard Zinn was a White historian, playwright, activist, and author, the son of Jewish immigrants who met as factory workers. He spent time as chair of the history department at Spelman College and as a professor at Boston University. He is known best for his activism concerning racial issues and for his 1980 book, *A People's History of the United States.*[5] Zinn founded the Zinn Education Project, which continues to challenge how history and the climate struggle get taught, particularly with regard to rethinking Columbus.

models in our society for what it looks like to be White in those three ways. Dr. Tatum says that for White people who want to be anti-racist, it's important to see what that looks like when other White people are doing it.

In this part of the chapter, we offer a portrait of a White anti-racist role model, Howard Zinn, a historian and committed activist. In his autobiography, *You Can't Be Neutral on a Moving Train*, he wrote, "We don't have to wait for some grand utopian future. The future is an endless succession of presents, and to live now as we think humans should live, in defiance of all that is bad around us, is itself a marvelous victory."[6]

Find other role models. This might include someone at your school or work who is a few years ahead of you. It could include White people in the news or White people throughout history. Look up some of the following names if you don't already know them: Kyle Korver, Anne Braden, Peter Norman, Grace Lee Boggs, John Brown, Lucretia Mott, Mab Segrest, Julius Waties Waring. For a more complete list, see the article "White Anti-Racist Activists" on the blog *Teaching While White*.[7]

Combat the Underlying Ideologies

Think again about some of the ideologies that underlie a racial hierarchy: individualism and meritocracy. Think about ways that you could shift from an individualistic mindset to a community mindset.

Think about how you could shift from a mindset that reinforces meritocracy to one of equity, how you could value every human being regardless of how much money they have, where they went to school, how many AP classes they took, whether they are thin or considered attractive, whether they are on the starting string of their sports team, whether they play sports at all. Think of the hierarchies all around you and how they place an artificial value on the human beings who make up your world. It doesn't mean you cannot value others' achievements. It just means that you don't value one person's humanity more than another's because of their achievements—or because of the privilege that helped make those achievements possible.

Remember that racism is not a zero-sum game. As Heather McGhee has written in *The Sum of Us*, racism hurts everyone. And when we work to dismantle racism, it helps everyone. McGhee gives the example in her book of public swimming pools in the South that were closed after desegregation because White people chose to have no pools at all rather than swim with Black people. In city after city, mayors and city managers filled brand-new, state-of-the-art pools with cement. This is just one of many examples McGhee lists about how racism costs everybody. And it is why anti-racism and racial justice benefit everyone. Look for Heather McGhee on the *Daily Show* with Trevor Noah to hear her tell you in her own words.[8]

Others

Throughout this book, we have included "Yeah, but . . ." statements. We hope you have found them useful. As you go forward, one way to increase your agility is to keep asking your own questions. But try this modification: change "Yeah, but . . ." to "Yes, *and*. . . ." The words "Yeah, but . . ." have a way of challenging the speaker, asking them to defend themselves, casting doubt or disagreement on what they are saying. Like playing the devil's advocate, it feels more

adversarial than collaborative. "Yes, and . . ." is a strategy from improv theater. It is a way of taking in what others are saying, affirming that you heard it, and then bringing your honest and authentic self to the conversation by sharing the questions that come up for you—not to challenge, but to learn.

Talk to other White people about race and racism. Remember those stories about backstage racism? When you're "backstage" and you hear White people making offensive jokes, making assumptions about People of Color, or operating as if we live in an all-White world, find ways to speak up and voice your resistance.

Sometimes White people compete to be the best anti-racist. This is a funny tendency that is related to how we rank people in US society (individualism!). Even as White people try to challenge that ranking by working for racial justice, they still might compete in the rankings to be the best anti-racist. The tendency to compete is related to performative anti-racism. Remember—you don't challenge racism by being better than the White person next to you. You challenge racism by helping other White people (and yourself) recognize racism and intervene with it. If you intervene with White people in a way that invites collaboration (rather than competing with them), you may be more successful at helping them rethink their assumptions over the long term, rather than just interrupting one snide comment.

What does that look like? First, be mindful of a common tendency for White people to intervene with one another in ways that are shaming rather than helpful. In their eagerness to avoid appearing racist—or to appear anti-racist—White people will often try to find the racism in the people around them and point it out—so that they themselves look good. Rather than competing to be the better White person, consider the other White person a potential ally—someone who can also be anti-racist if they get the right combination of support and challenge.

When you intervene with other White people, try this simple trick: *support* then *challenge*. In other words, support the person. Let them know something good that you've seen them do. Affirm their intention. Then challenge the comment or the behavior. Name it. Say why it offends you. Point out why it's a behavior that maintains a racial hierarchy.

Here's an example: "I appreciate you. You're always showing up to meetings early, making sure people have something to drink. You seem very thoughtful about others. So it hurts me when I hear you make that joke about Indian cab drivers. I just don't find it funny, and it doesn't seem consistent with who you seem to be."

If the person rejects your feedback by defending themselves, don't accuse them of being fragile. Don't walk away. Make yourself soft so that you can absorb the resistance. This is what Howard Stevenson calls racial jiu jitsu. Provide space for them to process feedback, take it in, and really feel it. Realize that you might be challenging a long-standing belief of theirs, and it may take a few minutes (or days or weeks) for that to sink in. Let them know you understand how frustrating it can be to have our viewpoints questioned. Hear them out. And then state again what you believe. Absorb the resistance, and then send the energy back to them in a transformed state.

Your goal here is to help the person take in the feedback and then continue to be open to anti-racist learning. Too often what happens is that White people get feedback, and then they become stunned, they fight back, or they disengage from the conversation. They literally go into fight, flight, freeze mode. Is this white fragility? Definitely. But as we have discussed, white fragility is a predictable reaction to growing up White within a racial hierarchy. It's common and widespread.

What many White people need in order to move from fragility to agility is practice engaging, engaging, and staying engaged. As another White person who is also engaged in unlearning the racial hierarchy, you can give them some space to process feedback, to take it in, to feel all the feels that come with it. You can walk with them on their journey to support their learning. In that way, hopefully you support other White people to be anti-racist for the long haul. Because it's not enough for every school or every workplace to have one really excellent, skilled White anti-racist who calls out everyone else and becomes the race police. If you are that person, hold steady! You are needed. But know that you cannot do this alone. And you are not immune from making mistakes; nobody is. Set about helping other White people to take the next step in their own journeys. Change happens when a critical mass of White people begin to unlearn the racial hierarchy and challenge the beliefs and practices that come with it. That's what it looks like to begin to change the system.

Model Your Own Efforts

Remember that the modeling you provide to peers can often be more powerful than any direct teaching or feedback. Being transparent and self-reflective about your own racial foibles and learning can help people see how to hold themselves accountable. When we've made mistakes, we can admit it and work it out in front of other White people who are trying to be anti-racist. It's not just about calling others out, but also being able to admit our own struggles and give others opportunities to support/challenge us. Show others what it looks like to take feedback without getting defensive. This simple action of holding yourself to your own standards of learning about racism and being open to seeing your bias can be such an important form of action. Asking for help from others is one of the quickest ways to build trust and be seen as credible.

Be an Ally, Not Just a Friend

Many years ago, I started to realize the difference between an ally and a friend. I had friends whom I liked, who liked me, but who did not share my same commitment to racial justice. When I tried to hold myself accountable for mixing up the names of two of my Black students, one of my White friends said, "Oh, Ali. You didn't mean anything by it. You're fine. You're the least racist person I know!" My White allies, on the other hand, helped me hold myself accountable. They wouldn't punish me or shame me, but they would relate to my

*disappointment, my frustration, my sadness. They
would help me think through the situation and
strategize about how to avoid doing it again. They
held me in loving accountability and helped me hold
myself accountable in a way that was supportive,
not shaming.* —Ali

Because white fragility is a predictable condition of growing up White within a racial hierarchy, it's important to be and to have White allies who are more than friends. Of course your allies can be your friends too. But your allies have a similar commitment to working on their own bias, to undoing racism, to dismantling the racial hierarchy. They will support you when you are feeling frustrated or confused. They will help you think through questions or role-play responses to racist comments you've heard. They won't shame you, but nor will they try to convince you that you shouldn't hold yourself to a high standard or that racist jokes are funny. They will help you figure out why the racist joke is racist, and help you figure out how to explain that to others.

When you have White allies you can rely on, you build a team that can help you practice. And you also ease the burden on Friends and Colleagues of Color who won't always be available to teach you or listen to your struggles. Although some Friends and Colleagues of Color may be willing to do that for you sometimes, it's too much to ask that they take on your growth and development as a personal project. In this day and age, many People of Color are saturated with their own feelings and others' feelings about racism. When White people find support in other White people for dealing with their feelings about racism, they are more able to show up to their relationships with People of Color for collaboration and connection, rather than out of a need for validation or a desire for teaching.

Your Sphere of Influence

Some people say, "There are so many things that need to happen, so many aspects of our lives that are shaped by racism. It starts to feel hopeless. What can I contribute?"

Think of it this way: if everyone worked within their own sphere of influence to make change, much would be different as a result. Think about where your passions and talents lie. Think about how racism impacts areas of your life where you have some influence or sway. This might include a club you are in or a team you're on. Pick an issue within that sphere, and consider how you could increase racial equity concerning that issue. Maybe you can propose that the French club study countries that have French as a national language and are home to predominantly People of Color. Learn the history of how those countries came to speak French, their legacy of colonialism, and how it affects the lives of the people who live there today. Find a way to share what you learn with peers.

Or if you play lacrosse, you could learn about the origin of the sport in Native cultures and about how Native youth today struggle to gain admission to national and international lacrosse competitions.[9] Look for ways your team might support those efforts. Find ways to be in solidarity with People of Color and Indigenous people by building connections, learning how their group has been impacted by history, and seeking ways to support their current efforts. Don't feel that you have to do everything.

Remember that whatever you do, it will be incomplete. Racism is big. As historian Isabel Wilkerson has pointed out, the US had enslavement for 246 years and has been without enslavement for 156 years. The first number will not be smaller than the second until after the year 2111.[10] Our country is still shaped by that legacy. But don't be discouraged, because everything you do to challenge the racial hierarchy helps. It is going to take a lot of people over several generations doing what they can, and then passing the baton, to continue to shift our country toward one that operates without a racial hierarchy. The journey you are on is one that will hopefully be integrated into your entire life, and the actions you take will differ as your knowledge, practice, and spheres of influence change.

Establish what you stand for, what you want to work for. Often we are so clear about what we are against that we don't know how to work for positive action. Consider Stacey Abrams, who lost the election for governor of Georgia in a race that many people believe was unfair. Look at how she turned around and created a voting-rights organization that mobilized voters (primarily working-class People of Color) who had not been counted on as a consistent voting block in decades. Work *for* something, not just *against* something.

Create space for the voices of People of Color to be heard. Creating space does not mean that you should be silent, or that you should be invisible. Some White people, in an attempt to take up less space, simply bow out. Don't bow out. Step forward boldly in an anti-racist way to imagine with other anti-racist people how to change the status quo. Build something new. Start an anti-racist book or film study group.

Join committees, and ensure that they have diverse representation. Ask, "Who is missing from this table, group, textbook, or celebration?" In meetings, discussions, and conversations, notice whose voices are being heard and whose aren't, and find ways to include them. When policy decisions are being made, see that they have taken into account the range of people who will be impacted by those decisions, and how.

Environmental activist Joanna Macy talks about how we can't transform society simply by tearing down what is. That action won't matter if we don't have an alternative. We also need to build new models so that others can see what is possible. Work in solidarity with others to show—even on an individual level—what's possible when we break down the racial hierarchy and build up a model of collective, cooperative, mutual support and respect. Show what's possible when such a powerful group takes action together.

We understand that it can be confusing when you don't want to engage in performative activism or draw attention to yourself, but you still want to do something. Flip-flopping between performative anti-racism and fear of looking inert becomes like a table-tennis game that can leave a person immobilized by inaction. Remember, it's not possible to be perfect. Instead of trying to look perfect, stay open to feedback, and self-reflect on how you're showing up. Approach anti-racist action with a combination of swagger and humility. Know that you cannot create change all by yourself. Know that bringing other people along with you is part of the task. Be humble enough to keep learning, keep asking for feedback. In your humility, you can model for other White people what it looks like to keep challenging racist ideas around you and in yourself. But when there is a moment to speak up, speak confidently. Be bold. Know that you are working toward a world where every person gets to show up and be their full self. Say your piece. Then listen some more.

Remember our dedication at the beginning of this book? We dedicate this book to young people because we know you can change the world. That is not just a euphemism. We mean it, and we know you can do it. When we meet you, we are going to ask, "What systems did you challenge today?"

Afterthoughts

DISCUSSION

Discuss the suggestions for continuing the work of anti-racism. What will be most challenging for you? How can you meet those challenges?

ACTIVITY

With a friend, practice responding to the following statement using an anti-racist lens: "You just want me to feel bad and guilty about something that I had nothing to do with." Use what you have learned from this book!

Journal

At the end of the original *White Fragility*, Robin lists a set of assumptions that she suggests White people work to internalize (repeated below). Choose five that you want to work on. Write about your plan for doing so.

- Being good or bad is not relevant.
- Racism is complex, and when I get feedback, I don't have to understand every nuance of the feedback to validate it.

- Bias is implicit and unconscious; I don't expect to be aware of mine without a lot of ongoing effort and help from others.
- Authentic anti-racism is rarely comfortable. Discomfort is key to my growth.
- I must not confuse comfort with safety. I am safe in conversations about race.
- I am not just an individual; I am also a member of a racial group, and I bring my group's history with me. History matters.
- Nothing exempts me from the forces of racism.
- Racism hurts (even kills) People of Color 24-7. Interrupting it is more important than my feelings, ego, or self-image.
- The antidote to guilt is taking action.

ACKNOWLEDGMENTS

We are forever grateful to all the students that worked with us on this project—some as pre-readers and focus group participants, and others whom we have learned from since before these ideas made it to these pages. Sudan Green, Sam Valerio-Sacks, Meqai Herder, Ahngelica Watson, Bridget Warleá, Erica Groomes, Morgan Burrell, Ayannah Woods, Bea Guerra, Abby Bekele, Tatiana Lee, Briana Butler, Bella Robinson, Nyeema Caldwell, Sofia Rodriguez-Burno, Nyasia Arrington, Laine May, Ahmaad Fulton, Himma Akiliu, Izzy Ebede, Lucy Kelley, Rachel Yakobashvili, Carly Shanken, Marina Garagozzo, Dalia Bender, Ben Borgman-Winter, Ben Shuster, Anya Hutter, Vin Manta, Tim Israel, Sarah Nourie, Madison Tillman, Rebecca Fisher, Elena Milliken, CC Servon, Annie Rupertus, Lucy Rupertus, Jed Panza, Olivia Avery, Jeremy Good, Zack Gharrafi, Ava Klebanoff, Kayla Alston, and Zion Todd.

We would like to thank Robin DiAngelo for her partnership. The trust that you granted us to rework the ideas and concepts from the original book has been such a gift.

We would like to thank our portrait artist, Kevin Soltau, and our illustrator, Lauren Kinnard, for your creativity and talent, which make this book come alive.

We would like to send thanks to the administration at Abington Friends School, who saw that it was necessary to create a program that brought us (Ali and Toni) together. The two of us met only a few times before taking a spontaneous road trip to New York City that became the foundation for a friendship that is now ten years old. Our friendship makes this work challenging and fun and easier and harder and joyful and meaningful and impactful and . . . all the things. May all our readers find a true partner in this work as we have found in one another.

To our team at The Race Institute for K–12 Educators. You support teachers in the long-term and personal work of building a strong, healthy racial identity so that they can help their students do the same. We are grateful for how you show up for teachers, long weekend after long weekend, and we are grateful to be with you on this journey.

In addition to our student readers, we would like to thank the friends and scholars who pre-read our work and/or gave us supportive and challenging ideas: Malik Mubashshir, Wendy Thompson, Mary Lynn Ellis, Chris Gunnin, Ian Lockey, Mary Conger, Frances Ramberg, Karen Shaffran, and Kendall Evans.

We thank everyone at Beacon Press who agreed to work on this project, for which there was no template. We appreciate your vision, your collaboration, and your trust.

Finally, we thank our families for their love and support, which make it possible for us to wake up and keep hope alive on a daily basis. Thank you to our children (both biological and in spirit), who inspire us and help us to believe in a better future.

Below we have listed a number of resources to help you continue your journey. None of these will say it all. We recommend that you read widely and listen widely, seeking out books, talks, and podcasts that center people other than your identity group. Listen to the voices of people who are different from you to get a window onto experiences that are different from your own—and also onto things you have in common. Excellent new books, blogs, and podcasts come out all the time that we still don't know about; maybe you will create them. We hope that some of the resources here will help you take your next steps.

Nonfiction Books

Me and White Supremacy: Combat Racism, Change the World, and Become a Good Ancestor, by Layla F. Saad

A Queer History of the United States for Young People, by Michael Bronshi, adapted by Richie Chevat

Our Stories, Our Voices: 21 YA Authors Get Real About Injustice, Empowerment, and Growing Up Female in America, edited by Amy Reed

Lies My Teacher Told Me: Everything American History Textbooks Get Wrong, Young Readers' Edition, by James W. Loewen, adapted by Rebecca Stefoff

An Indigenous People's History of the United States for Young People, by Roxanne Dunbar-Ortiz, adapted by Jean Mendoza and Debbie Reese

A Young People's History of the United States, Volume One by Howard Zinn, adapted by Rebecca Stefoff

A Young People's History of the United States, Volume Two, by Howard Zinn, adapted by Rebecca Stefoff

A Different Mirror for Young People: A History of Multicultural America, by Ronald Takaki, adapted by Rebecca Stefoff

Stamped: Racism, Antiracism, and You: A Remix of Stamped from the Beginning, by Jason Reynolds and Ibram X. Kendi

Rising Out of Hatred: The Awakening of a Former White Nationalist, by Eli Saslow

You Mean There's Race in My Movie?: The Complete Guide to Understanding Race in Mainstream Hollywood, 2nd ed., by Frederick W. Gooding Jr.

True or False: A CIA Analyst's Guide to Spotting Fake News, by Cindy L. Otis

This Book Is Anti-Racist: 20 Lessons on How to Wake Up, Take Action, and Do the Work, by Tiffany Jewell

They Called Us Enemy, by George Takei, Justin Eisinger, and Steven Scott

March (Books 1–3), by John Lewis and Andrew Aydin

The Birchbark House Series, by Louise Erdrich

The 1619 Project: A New Origin Story, created by Nikole Hannah-Jones

Our Time Is Now, by Stacey Abrams

The Immortal Life of Henrietta Lacks, by Rebecca Skloot

Sigh, Gone, by Phuc Tran

Good Talk, by Mira Jacob

Is Everyone Really Equal? An Introduction to Key Concepts in Social Justice Education, by Özlem Sensoy and Robin DiAngelo

Blog

Microaggressions.com

Videos and Talks

Jay Smooth, "How I Learned to Stop Worrying and Love Discussing Race," TEDx Hampshire College, November 15, 2011, www.youtube.com/watch?v=MbdxeFcQtaU

Aamer Rahman, "Fear of a Brown Planet," November 28, 2013, www.youtube.com/watch?v=dw_mRaIHb-M

David Lammy, "Climate Justice Can't Happen Without Racial Justice," TED Countdown, October 2020, www.ted.com/talks/david_lammy_climate_justice_can_t_happen_without_racial_justice?language=en

Heather McGhee and Trevor Noah, "The Sum of Us and the True Cost of Racism," *The Daily Social Distancing Show*, February 18, 2021, www.youtube.com/watch?v=IZpse-90KTY

Heather McGhee, "Racism Has a Cost for Everyone," TED Talk, May 8, 2020, www.youtube.com/watch?v=eaCrsBtiYA4

Films

Race: The Power of an Illusion (2003), a three-part documentary series produced by California Newsreel

A Class Divided (1985), produced by *Frontline*

Podcasts

Nice White Parents
Scene on Radio: Seeing White
Throughline
The Improvement Association
Climate Cuisine
Code Switch

Organizations

We Need Diverse Books, https://diversebooks.org

American Library Association, www.ala.org/advocacy/diversity

Keep It In the Ground, www.ienearth.org/keepitintheground/

Stop the Line 3 Pipeline, www.stopline3.org

National Native American Boarding School Healing Coalition, https://boardingschoolhealing.org

Learning for Justice, www.learningforjustice.org/magazine

US vs. Hate, https://usvshate.org

United States Holocaust Memorial Museum, www.ushmm.org

Transgender Training Institute, www.transgendertraininginstitute.com

Project 562: Changing the Way we See Native America, www.project562.com

Colorlines, www.colorlines.com

Fiction Books

Kindred: A Graphic Novel, by Octavia E. Butler
Parable of the Sower, by Octavia E. Butler

The City We Became, by N. K. Jemisin

The Gilded Ones, by Nnedi Okorafor

Americanah, by Chimamanda Ngozi Adichie

Another Brooklyn, by Jacqueline Woodson

American Born Chinese, by Gene Luen Yang

Dragon Hoops, by Gene Luen Yang

New Kid and *Class Act*, by Jerry Craft

The Only Black Girls in Town, by Brandy Colbert

Black Brother, Black Brother, by Jewell Parker Rhodes

Blended, by Sharon M. Draper

The Poet X, by Elizabeth Acevedo

The Hate U Give, by Angie Thomas

Pet, by Akwaeke Emezi

Long Way Down, by Jason Reynolds

Piecing Me Together, by Renée Watson

All American Boys, by Jason Reynolds and Brendan Kiely

Angel of Greenwood, by Randi Pink

A Song Below Water, by Bethany C. Morrow

Who Put This Song On?, by Morgan Parker

You Should See Me in a Crown, by Leah Johnson

Dear Haiti, Love Alaine, by Maika Moulite and Maritza Moulite

Felix Ever After, by Kacen Callender

Hearts Unbroken, by Cynthia Leitich Smith

Interior Chinatown, by Charles Wu

NOTES

HOW TO READ THIS BOOK

1. Glenn E. Singleton and Curtis Linton, *Courageous Conversations About Race: A Field Guide for Achieving Equity in Schools*, 2nd ed. (Thousand Oaks, CA: Corwin Press, 2007), 74.

CHAPTER 1

1. The above quote comes from Isabel Wilkerson, *Caste: The Origins of Our Discontents* (New York: Random House, 2020), 50.
2. Ibid., 17.
3. Ibid., 19.
4. Frederick Gooding Jr., ed., *The Minority Reporter: You Mean There's Race in My Movie?* (Silver Spring, MD: On the Reelz Press, 2007).
5. R. Rothstein, *The Color of Law: A Forgotten History of How Our Government Segregated America* (New York: Liveright Publishing, 2017).
6. Pages Matam, Elizabeth Acevedo, and G. Yamazawah, "Unforgettable," posted September 4, 2014, www.youtube.com /watch?v=Xvah3E1fP20.
7. "Race and Ethnicity of Public School Teachers and Their Students" (2017–2018 school year), Data Point, US Department of Education Statistics, National Center for Education Statistics, September 2020, https://nces.ed.gov/pubs2020/2020103/index.asp.
8. When we talk about power that comes from group membership, we are talking about social power/rank. According to

psychologist Arnold Mindell, social power is different from institutional power/rank or spiritual power/rank. Arnold Mindell, *Sitting in the Fire* (San Francisco: Deep Democracy Exchange, 2014).

9. The terms "nondisabled" and "disabled" might sound a little strange, especially if you are used to the identity-first language of people with disabilities. However, these terms are widely and most commonly preferred in disability-justice and disability-rights communities. "Able-bodied" is being retired because it suggests that disabled people aren't able bodied.

10. Thank you to social-justice activist Rodney Glasgow for this framing.

CHAPTER 2

1. Beverly Daniel Tatum, *Why Are All the Black Kids Sitting Together in the Cafeteria?* (New York: Basic Books, 2017).

2. "Slavery at Monticello," Thomas Jefferson Monticello, accessed September 29, 2021, www.monticello.org/slavery/?ref =homeblock.

3. Ta-Nehisi Coates, *Between the World and Me* (New York: Spiegel and Grau, 2015).

4. Ibid.

5. "What Census Calls Us: A Historical Timeline," Pew Research Center, accessed November 1, 2021, www.pewresearch.org/wp -content/uploads/2020/02/PH_15.06.11_MultiRacial-Timeline .pdf.

6. Ian Haney López, *White by Law: Tenth Anniversary Edition* (New York: New York University Press, 2006).

7. Ibid.

8. Eli Saslow, *Rising Out of Hatred: The Awakening of a Former White Nationalist* (New York: Anchor Books, 2017).

9. "The Year in Hate 2019: White Nationalist Groups Rise for a Second Year in a Row—Up 55% Since 2017," Southern Poverty Law Center, press release, March 18, 2020, www.splcenter .org/presscenter/year-hate-2019-white-nationalist-groups-rise -second-yearrow-55-2017.

10. Ibid.

11. *New Hate and Old: The Changing Face of American White Supremacy: A Report from the Center on Extremism*, Anti-Defamation League, Accessed December 28, 2021, www.adl.org /media/11894/download.

12. Michael Edison Hayden, "Neo-Nazi Website Daily Stormer Is 'Designed to Target Children' as Young as 11 for Radicalization, Editor Claims," *Newsweek*, January 16, 2018, www.newsweek.com/website-daily-stormer-designed-target -children-editor-claims-782401.

13. Marilyn Frye, *The Politics of Reality: Essays in Feminist Theory* (Trumansburg, NY: Crossing Press, 1983).

14. Amy Stuart Wells, Lauren Fox, and Diana Cordova-Cobo, *How Racially Diverse Schools and Classrooms Can Benefit All Students*, Century Foundation, February 9, 2016, https://tcf.org /content/report/how-racially-diverse-schools-and-classrooms -can-benefit-all-students/?agreed=1&session=1&session=1& agreed=1; Patricia Y. Gurin, Eric L. Dey, Gerald Gurin, and Sylvia Hurtado, "How Does Racial/Ethnic Diversity Promote Education?," *Western Journal of Black Studies* 27, no. 1 (2003): 20.

15. Tim Wise, *Affirmative Action: Racial Preference in Black and White* (New York: Routledge, 2005).

16. Denise Lu, Jon Huang, Ashwin Seshagiri, Haeyoun Park, and Troy Griggs, "Faces of Power: 80% Are White, Even as U.S. Becomes More Diverse," *New York Times*, September 9, 2020, https://www.nytimes.com/interactive/2020/09/09/us/powerful -people-race-us.html.

17. Thomas Jefferson, *Notes on the State of Virginia; with Related Documents*, ed. David Waldstreicher (Boston: Bedford/ St. Martin's, 2002).

CHAPTER 3

1. Eduardo Bonilla-Silva, *Racism Without Racists: Color-Blind Racism and the Persistence of Racial Inequality in the United States*, 5th ed. (Lanham, MD: Rowman and Littlefield, 2006).

2. Deborah Hill, "Eduardo Bonilla-Silva: The Strange Career of a Race Scholar," *Duke Today*, May 8, 2018, https://today.duke .edu/2018/05/eduardo-bonilla-silva-strange-career-race-scholar.

3. Beverly Daniel Tatum, *Why Are All the Black Kids Sitting Together in the Cafeteria?* (New York: Basic Books, 2017).

4. "Legal Highlight: The Civil Rights Act of 1964," US Department of Labor, Office of the Assistant Secretary for Administration and Management, accessed September 29, 2021, www.dol.gov/agencies/oasam/civil-rights-center/statutes /civil-rights-act-of-1964.

5. Howard Zinn, adapted by Rebecca Stefoff, *A Young People's History of the United States*, vol. 2 (New York: Seven Stories Press, 2007).

6. This concept comes from the distinction between "racial" and "racist" put forth in Michael Omi and Howard Winant, *Racial Formation in the United States*, 3rd ed. (New York: Routledge Press, 2015).

7. Tracy Jan, "White Families Have Nearly Ten Times the Net Worth of Black Families. And the Gap Is Growing," *Washington Post*, September 28, 2017, www.washingtonpost .com/news/wonk/wp/2017/09/28/black-and-hispanic-families -are-making-more-money-but-they-still-lag-far-behind-whites/.

8. More on this in Chapter 6.

9. Adam R. Pearson, John F. Dovidio, and Samuel L. Gaertner, "The Nature of Contemporary Prejudice: Insights from Aversive Racism," *Social and Personality Psychology Compass* 3, no. 3 (May 2009), https://doi.org/10.1111/j.1751-9004.2009 .00183.x. In the original study, White participants were divided into categories called "prejudiced" (i.e., high in both explicit and implicit prejudice), "non-prejudiced" (i.e., low in both explicit and implicit prejudice), and "aversive racists" (i.e., low in explicit prejudice, but high in implicit prejudice), which we tend to call "non-racist." We change the language here to be consistent with the language we use throughout the book.

10. J. F. Dovidio, "On the Nature of Contemporary Prejudice: The Third Wave," *Journal of Social Issues* 57 (2001): 829–49;

J. F. Dovidio, S. L. Gaertner, K. Kawakami, and G. Hodson, "Why Can't We Just Get Along? Interpersonal Biases and Interracial Distrust," *Cultural Diversity and Ethnic Minority Psychology* 8 (2002a): 88–102; J. F. Dovidio, K. Kawakami, and S. L. Gaertner, "Implicit and Explicit Prejudice and Interracial Interaction," *Journal of Personality and Social Psychology* 82 (2002b): 62–68.

11. A recent study shows that Black people and Brown people face 56 percent and 63 percent more exposure to air pollution than their consumption generates, while White people face 17 percent less exposure to air pollution than their consumption generates. Isaac Stanley-Becker, "Whites Are Mainly to Blame for Air Pollution, but Blacks and Hispanics Bear the Burden, Says a New Study," *Washington Post*, March 12, 2019, www.washingtonpost .com/nation/2019/03/12/whites-are-mainly-blame-air-pollution -blacks-hispanics-bear-burden-says-new-study/.

12. "Asthma and African Americans," Office of Minority Health, US Department of Health and Human Services, last modified February 11, 2021, https://minorityhealth.hhs.gov/omh/browse .aspx?lvl=4&lvlid=15.

13. We encourage you to listen to David Lammy's talk on TED Countdown, "Climate Justice Can't Happen Without Racial Justice," October 2020, www.ted.com/talks/david_lammy _climate_justice_can_t_happen_without_racial_justice#t-555897.

14. Caleb Okereke and Stephanie Busari, "She Was Cropped Out of a Photo of White Climate Activists. Now, She Says It's Time to Stop Erasing African Voices," CNN, updated February 5, 2020, www.cnn.com/2020/01/30/africa/uganda-activist-vanessa -nakate-cropped-intl/index.html.

15. Nick Morrison, "It's GPAs, Not Standardized Tests, That Predict College Success," *Forbes*, January 29, 2020, https://www .forbes.com/sites/nickmorrison/2020/01/29/its-gpas-not-stand ardized-tests-that-predict-college-success/?sh=407ddb7c32bd.

16. Toni Morrison, "On the Backs of Blacks," *Time*, December 2, 1993, http://content.time.com/time/magazine/article /0,9171,979736,00.html.

17. Update to Toni's story: Twenty-five years after the conversation with my college roommate about our SAT and ACT scores, we are still in touch. We've remained friends, which now looks like a Christmas card exchange and a marathon phone call once a year or so. In our hundreds of conversations, we've never returned to the one where she asked, "How did you get in?"—until I decided to include that story in this book. My college roommate and I have been talking more often since the murder of George Floyd. Because she lives near Minneapolis, Minnesota, that event hit close to home for her, literally. She has never shied away from deep conversations, but that tragedy pushed her into a reckoning with race and racism much like the one the rest of the country has gone through. She has asked me for advice on what to read and what workshops to attend, and she has asked for my thoughts on raising her three White kids to be racially conscious. So I had no doubt that when this book hits the shelves she will want to read it.

I started thinking about what it might be like for her while reading this book to come upon that story. I decided to tell her that I'd included it. What happened next was transformative for our friendship. She told me she is glad I shared the story because she would be happy for someone to learn from her mistakes. She apologized appropriately for what had happened all those years ago. And then she replayed the conversation—except this time from her point of view.

We remembered the same words, but she remembered her intent. She actually saw the conversation as a bonding moment. We were two girls who didn't fit the mold at a big ol' elite university. How did we "sneak" in? She was a country girl from Minnesota who was admitted as a Division I athlete. So she wanted to know how I sneaked in. She understands now that the reason she didn't fit in had nothing to do with her being White, and that her navigating those differences over the years was not clouded by the burden of systemic racism. The importance of intent and impact has not been lost on her. In an email she wrote, "Your feelings and your interpretations of my actions are more important than my intent. I'm sorry for the burdens I placed on you with the mistakes I made along the way and for those I continue to make today. I'm trying very hard to continue to learn and grow." I loved getting that email and have read it over and over. The importance of the relationship we have built over the years finally led us to this conversation. Imagine if we had possessed the skills to engage in this type of discussion twenty-five years ago!

My hope (and hers) is that those of you who are reading this are able to reach that place much faster than we did. She wrote something else that I will not forget: "Some day I aspire to be mentioned as an example of success." Here ya go, roomie.—Toni

18. Leslie H. Picca and Joe R. Feagin, *Two-Faced Racism: Whites in the Backstage and Frontstage* (New York: Taylor and Francis, 2007).

CHAPTER 4

1. Ijeoma Oluo, "White People: I Don't Want You to Understand Me Better, I Want You to Understand Yourselves," Medium, February 7, 2017, https://medium.com/the-establishment/white -people-i-dont-want-you-to-understand-me-better-i-want-you -to-understand-yourselves-a6fbedd42ddf.

2. Emily Style, "Curriculum as Window and Mirror," *Social Science Record* 33, no. 2 (1996): 21–28.

3. Ruth Frankenberg, *White Women, Race Matters: The Social Construction of Whiteness* (Minneapolis: University of Minnesota Press, 1993), 1.

4. Zeam Porter with Ty Gale, "Blackness/Transness: Two Targets on my Back," in *The Guide for White Women who Teach Black Boys* (Thousand Oaks, CA: Corwin Press, 2017), 204–209.

5. Eli Green of the Teaching Transgender Institute suggests that trans students need exposure to twelve to fourteen out, visible trans teachers or out, visible trans ally teachers in order to mitigate the negative effects of transphobia they experience in school.

6. "Chinese Exclusion Act," History.com, September 13, 2017, www.history.com/topics/immigration/chinese-exclusion-act-1882.

7. Maria Godoy, "In US Cities, the Health Effects of Past Housing Discrimination Are Plain to See," National Public Radio, November 19, 2020, www.npr.org/sections/health-shots/2020/11/19/911909187/in-u-s-cities-the-health-effects-of-past-housing-discrimination-are-plain-to-see.

8. Richard Rothstein, "A 'Forgotten History' of How the U.S. Government Segregated America," interview by Terry Gross, *Fresh Air*, NPR, May 3, 2017, www.npr.org/2017/05/03/526655831/a-forgotten-history-of-how-the-u-s-government-segregated-america.

9. Svati Kirsten Narula, "The Real Problem with a Service Called 'Ghetto Tracker,'" *The Atlantic*, September 6, 2013, www.theatlantic.com/technology/archive/2013/09/the-real-problem-with-a-service-called-ghetto-tracker/279403/.

10. Michelle Alexander, *The New Jim Crow: Mass Incarceration in the Age of Colorblindness*, 10th anniv. ed. (New York: New Press, 2012).

11. "James Baldwin: 'I Am Not Your Negro' Dick Cavett Show—1968," June 13, 1968, video, Speakola.com, https://speakola.com/ideas/james-baldwin-i-am-not-your-negro-dick-cavett-show.

12. Heather Long and Andrew Van Dam, "The Black-White Economic Divide Is as Wide as It Was in 1968," *Washington Post*, June 4, 2020, www.washingtonpost.com/business/2020/06/04/economic-divide-black-households/.

13. Alexander, *The New Jim Crow*.

14. Lynn Neary, "Victim of Brock Turner Sexual Assault Reveals Her Identity," NPR, September 4, 2019, www.npr.org/2019/09/04/757626939/victim-of-brock-turner-sexual-assault-reveals-her-identity.

15. Michael E. Miller, "All-American Swimmer Found Guilty of Sexually Assaulting Unconscious Woman on Stanford Campus," *Washington Post*, March 31, 2016, www.washingtonpost.com

/news/morning-mix/wp/2016/03/31/all-american-swimmer
-found-guilty-of-sexually-assaulting-unconscious-woman-on
-stanford-campus/.

16. Alexander, *The New Jim Crow*.

17. See the work of Heather McGhee in *The Sum of Us: What Racism Costs Everyone and How We Can Prosper Together* to learn more about this topic.

CHAPTER 5

1. People also call it black/white thinking. We choose to call it either/or because we don't want to suggest that black and white are mutually exclusive categories in this discussion of race.

2. Michele Borba, "Mobilizing Bystanders to Stop Bullying," February 23, 2011, www.micheleborba.com/parenting-advice -parenting-tips/mobilizing-bystanders-to-stop-bullying-6 -teachable-skills-to-stop-a-bully/.

3. Carol Dweck, *Mindset: The New Psychology of Success* (New York: Ballantine Books, 2003).

4. Jay Smooth, "How I Learned to Stop Worrying and Love Discussing Race," TEDx Hampshire College, November 15, 2011, video, www.youtube.com/watch?v=MbdxeFcQtaU.

5. Carol Anderson, "Ferguson Isn't About Black Rage Against Cops. It's White Rage Against Progress," *Washington Post*, August 29, 2014, www.washingtonpost.com/opinions /ferguson-wasnt-black-rage-against-copsit-was-white-rage -against-progress/2014/08/29/3055e3f4-2d75-11e4-bb9b -997ae96fad33_story.html.

6. Carol Anderson, *White Rage: The Unspoken Truth of Our Racial Divide* (New York: Bloomsbury, 2016).

7. Ibid., 176.

CHAPTER 6

1. Nicholas Jones, Rachel Marks, Roberto Ramirez, and Merarys Ríos-Vargas, "2020 Census Illuminates Racial and Ethnic Composition of the Country," United States Census Bureau, August 12, 2021, www.census.gov/library/stories/2021

/08/improved-race-ethnicity-measures-reveal-united-states
-population-much-more-multiracial.html.

2. Glossary, Understanding Race: A Project of the Association of American Anthropologists, accessed December 29, 2021, https://understandingrace.org/Glossary#r.

3. Phillip Bump, "Use of 'Latinx' Is Low on the List of What Democrats Should Be Nervous About with Hispanic Voters," *Washington Post*, December 6, 2021.

4. Chimamanda Ngozi Adichie, *Americanah* (New York: Anchor Books, 2013), 129.

5. "Carnaval del Barrio," *In the Heights* (film), Jon M. Chu, dir., Warner Bros., 2021.

6. Bernardo M. Ferdman and Plácida I. Gallegos, "Racial Identity Development and Latinos in the United States," in *New Perspectives on Racial Identity Development*, ed. Charmaine L. Wijeyesinghe and Bailey W. Jackson III (New York: New York University Press, 2001), 38.

7. To learn more about the tribal nations recognized by the US government, see US Department of the Interior, Indian Affairs, Tribal Leaders Directory, accessed November 9, 2021, www .bia.gov/bia/ois/tribal-leaders-directory/; and US Department of the Interior, Indian Affairs, Frequently Asked Questions, accessed December 30, 2021, www.bia.gov/frequently-asked-questions.

8. "Tribal Nations and the United States: An Introduction," National Congress of American Indians, accessed December 30, 2021, https://ncai.org/about-tribes.

9. Isabel Wilkerson, *Caste: The Origins of Our Discontents* (New York: Random House, 2020).

10. Vivian Chou, "How Science and Genetics are Reshaping the Race Debate in the 21st Century," Harvard University Graduate School of Arts and Sciences, April 17, 2017, https:// sitn.hms.harvard.edu/flash/2017/science-genetics-reshaping-race -debate-21st-century/.

11. "Go Deeper: Race Timeline," *Race: The Power of an Illusion*, PBS.org, accessed October 1, 2021, www.pbs.org/race/000 _About/002_03_a-godeeper.htm.

12. "Jehovah's Witnesses," United States Holocaust Memorial Museum, accessed December 30, 2021, www.ushmm.org /collections/bibliography/jehovahs-witnesses.

13. Ian Haney López, *White by Law: 10th Anniversary Edition* (New York: New York University Press, 2006).

14. Maria P. P. Root, ed., *The Multiracial Experience: Racial Borders as the New Frontier*, (Thousand Oaks, CA: Sage Publishing, 1995).

15. We believe that all people—including White people—are negatively impacted by racism, but in very different ways. The term "People of Color" describes people who are excluded from the benefits of Whiteness within the racial hierarchy.

16. Amanda Morris, "What Is Settler Colonialism?," Learning for Justice, January 22, 2019, www.learningforjustice.org /magazine/what-is-settlercolonialism.

17. Associated Press, "Before Venezuela, US Had Long Involvement in Latin America," January 25, 2019, https://apnews.com/article /north-america-caribbean-ap-top-news-venezuela-honduras-2de d14659982426c9b2552827734be83.

18. Suzanne Gamboa, "Racism, Not a Lack of Assimilation, Is the Real Problem Facing Latinos in America," NBC News, February 26, 2019, www.nbcnews.com/news/latino/racism-not -lack-assimilation-real-problem-facing-latinos-america-n974021.

19. Based on the definition from Derald Wing Sue, Christina M. Capodilupo, Gina C. Torino, Jennifer M. Bucceri, Aisha Holder, Kevin L. Nadal, and Marta Esquilin, "Racial Microaggressions in Everyday Life: Implications for Clinical Practice," *American Psychologist* 62, no. 4 (2007): 271–286.

20. Ronald Takaki, *A Different Mirror: A History of Multicultural America* (New York: Back Bay Books, 2008), 192.

21. Sue et al., "Racial Microaggressions in Everyday Life," 271.

22. Derald Wing Sue, Jennifer Bucceri, Annie I. Lin, Kevin L. Nadal, and Gina C. Torino, "Racial Microaggressions and the Asian American Experience," *Cultural Diversity and Ethnic Minority Counseling* 13, no. 1 (2007): 72–81.

23. Stacey J. Lee, *Up Against Whiteness* (New York: Teachers College Press, 2005), 4.

24. Lee Anne Bell, "Theoretical Foundations for Social Justice Education," in *Teaching for Diversity and Social Justice*, ed. Maurianne Adams, Lee Anne Bell, and Pat Griffin (New York: Routledge, 2007), 10.

25. "US Indian Boarding School History," National Native American Boarding School Healing Coalition, accessed January 1, 2022, https://boardingschoolhealing.org/education /us-indian-boarding-school-history/.

26. "Kill the Indian, Save the Man: An Introduction to the History of Boarding Schools," National Native American Boarding School Healing Coalition, August 3, 2020, https:// boardingschoolhealing.org/kill-the-indian-save-the-man-an -introduction-to-the-history-of-boarding-schools/.

27. Keep It in the Ground News Archives, Indigenous Environmental Network, accessed December 30, 2021, https:// www.ienearth.org/keepitintheground/.

28. Stop the Line 3 Pipeline, accessed December 30, 2021, https:// www.stopline3.org.

29. Janice A. Sabin, "How We Fail Black Patients in Pain," Association of American Medical Colleges, January 6, 2020, www.aamc.org/news-insights/how-we-fail-black-patients-pain.

30. Tulsa Historical Society and Museum, "The Attack on Greenwood," accessed October 1, 2021, www.tulsahistory.org /exhibit/1921-tulsa-race-massacre/.

31. History.com Editors, "Loving v. Virginia," History.com, updated January 25, 2021, www.history.com/topics/civil-rights -movement/loving-v-virginia

32. Wilkerson, *Caste*, 109.

CHAPTER 7

1. What happened next is an example of what often occurs when White people have accountability conversations with each other about anti-racism. The teacher who used the n-word went to a White affinity space that was a part of the workshop design. The space was facilitated by a White workshop leader and was only for participants who identified as White. Of course,

I am not sure what was said, but I do know that when the teacher returned, the conversation we had was important to our relationship. She apologized for her actions and let me know that she understood the impact of her voice in that space and with her students. She vowed to be in solidarity with me at our school as we moved forward toward anti-racism. And she continues to be that ally many years later.

2. "Ta-Nehisi Coates on Words That Don't Belong to Everyone: We Were Eight Years in Power Book Tour," November 7, 2017, video, www.youtube.com/watch?v=QO15S3WC9pg.

3. "Children Notice Race Several Years Before Adults Want to Talk About It," American Psychological Association, November 27, 2020, www.apa.org/news/press/releases/2020/08/children-notice-race; and A. Dulin-Keita, L. Hannon, J. R. Fernandez, and W. C. Cockerham, "The Defining Moment: Children's Conceptualization of Race and Experiences with Racial Discrimination," *Ethnic and Racial Studies* 34, no. 4 (2011): 662–682, https://doi.org/10.1080/01419870.2011.535906.

4. Ruth Frankenberg, *White Women, Race Matters: The Social Construction of Whiteness* (Minneapolis: University of Minnesota Press, 1993), 1.

5. Although this terminology is widely used without a clear origin, it is often attributed to educator Elsie Y. Cross. It is taken here from Antje Mattheus and Lorraine Marino, *White People Confronting Racism: A Manual for a 3-Part Workshop*, 2nd ed. (Philadelphia: self-published, 2011).

6. E. Bonilla-Silva, Amanda Lewis, and David G. Embrick. "'I Did Not Get That Job Because of a Black Man . . .': The Story Lines and Testimonies of Color-Blind Racism," *Sociological Forum* 19, no. 4 (2004): 555–581, http://www.jstor.org/stable/4148829.

CHAPTER 8

1. To learn more about "calling in" versus "calling out," see Loretta J. Ross's TED talk, "Don't Call People Out—Call Them In," August 2021, www.ted.com/talks/loretta_j_ross_don_t_call_people_out_call_them_in.

CHAPTER 9

1. Brendesha M. Tynes, "Online Racial Discrimination: A Growing Problem for Adolescents," *Psychological Science Agenda*, December 2015, www.apa.org/science/about/psa/2015/12/online-racial-discrimination.

2. "New Survey Finds That 83 Percent of Teens Acknowledge That Systemic Racism Is an Issue and They Want to Be Included in the National Conversation Around Social Justice," 4-H, August 13, 2020, https://4-h.org/media/new-survey-finds-that-83-percent-of-teens-acknowledge-that-systemic-racism-is-an-issue-and-they-want-to-be-included-in-the-national-conversation-around-social-justice/.

3. Layla F. Saad, *Me and White Supremacy: Combat Racism, Change the World, and Become a Good Ancestor* (Naperville, IL, Sourcebooks, 2020), 74.

4. Cindy L. Otis, *True or False: A CIA Analysts' Guide to Spotting Fake News* (New York: Feiwel and Friends, 2020), 208–215.

5. Ibid., 257–266.

6. AAP, "Disney Princesses Outspoken by Males in Frozen, The Little Mermaid, Research Shows," *Sydney Morning Herald*, January 27, 2016, https://www.smh.com.au/entertainment/movies/disney-princesses-outspoken-by-males-in-frozen-the-little-mermaid-research-shows-20160126-gmefdc.html.

7. Frederick W. Gooding Jr., *You Mean There's Race in My Movie?: The Complete Guide to Understanding Race in Mainstream Hollywood*, 2nd ed. (Silver Spring, MD: On the Reelz Press, 2017).

8. Reprinted with permission from Frederick W. Gooding, Jr.

CHAPTER 10

1. Thank you to social-justice advocate and diversity practitioner Yvonne Adams for this concept and chapter title.

2. Nassim Nicholas Taleb, *Antifragile: Things That Gain from Disorder* (New York: Random House, 2012).

3. Howard Stevenson, "Recasting the Moment: Professor Howard Stevenson on Creating Change Through Racial

Literacy," interview by Juliana Rosati, Penn Graduate School of Education, October 22, 2020, www.gse.upenn.edu/news /recasting-moment-professor-howard-stevenson-creating-change -through-racial-literacy.

4. Beverly Daniel Tatum, *Why Are All the Black Kids Sitting Together in the Cafeteria?* (New York: Basic Books, 2017).

5. Howard Zinn, *A People's History of the United States* (New York: Harper and Row, 1990), 31.

6. Howard Zinn, *You Can't Be Neutral on a Moving Train* (Boston: Beacon Press, 2002).

7. Elizabeth Denevi and Lori Cohen, "White Anti-Racist Activists," *Teaching While White* (blog), accessed October 4, 2021, www.teachingwhilewhite.org/resources/white-antiracist -activists.

8. Heather McGhee, "The Sum of Us," interview by Trevor Noah, *The Daily Show*, Comedy Central, February 17, 2021, www .cc.com/video/rf6jea/the-daily-show-with-trevor-noah-heather -mcghee-the-sum-of-us.

9. Vincent Schilling, "The Creator's Game: Native People Created Lacrosse Yet Now Strive to Play the Sport in International Arenas," *American Indian Magazine*, Spring 2021, www .americanindianmagazine.org/story/the-creators-game.

10. Isabel Wilkerson, *Caste: The Origins of Our Discontents* (New York: Random House, 2020), 48.

INDEX

the same), 118–119; White-
people kryptonite, 112
Gooding, Frederick, Jr., 203
good old days, 88–90
*The Guide for White Women
Who Teach Black Boys*, 88

"head-in-the-sand" racism, 65
Home Owners' Loan
Corporation, 91
human ideal, depiction of White
people as, 15–16
hypodescent, law of, 135

ideologies, 17–19, 156
"I Have a Dream" speech (King),
56–58
"illegal alien," 140
Immigration and Nationality Act,
141
implicit bias, 63, 65, 230
Indigenous Environmental
Network, 145–146
intentional racism, 176
internalized superiority, 72, 156
*The Island at the Center of the
World*, 141

Jefferson, Thomas, 16, 33
Jim Crow South, 12, 47, 87
jokes, 75, 76, 200–202
justice system, 98, 99
Juveniles of Color, behavior of, 98

Kendi, Ibram X., 62, 70
King, Martin Luther, Jr., 1,
56, 57
KKK, 29, 41, 47, 176

Lammy, David, 67
Latinx people: microaggressions
against, 140; racism against,
139–141
law of hypodescent, 135
Lee, Stacey J., 143, 144
legacy admission (college), 72
Loving v. Virginia, 149

Macy, Joanna, 228
Martin, Trayvon, 92
McGhee, Heather, 220
*Me and White Supremacy:
Combat Racism, Change the
World, and Become a Good
Ancestor*, 190, 191
#MeAndWhiteSupremacy, 190
media analysis, 186–207;
costumes and jokes,
200–202; disagreeing on
social media, 189–190; fake
news, 195–197; People of
Color archetypes, 203–205;
performative activism,
193–195; recommendation
to White students, 189;
repurposing of content, 187;
social media, 187–189; social
media, being anti-racist
on, 189–192; social media,
dangers and benefits of,
197–200; Students of Color
survey results, 186; White
archetypes, 205–206; written
word, ambiguity of, 192–193
Mediocre, 80
melanin, 125
Menzies, Gavin, 141
meritocracy, 19, 156
Me Too movement, 190
microaggressions: against Asian
Americans, 142; against
Latinx people, 140; fear of
committing, 211; forms of,
141; racial, 141
Miller, Chanel, 97
Miranda, Lin-Manuel, 132
Morrison, Toni, 72
Muslims, people perceived
as, 126

Nakate, Vanessa, 68
Native people, colonization and,
144–146
neighborhoods, segregated, 14–15
neo-Nazis, 44

Sue, Derald Wing, 141, 142
The Sum of Us, 220
superiority: children's developed
    sense of, 161; internalized,
    72, 156; learned sense of,
    72; unconscious, 82; White,
    assumptions about, 15; White,
    White denial of, 161
supremacists and supremacy
    (racism and), 29–55;
    affirmative action, 52; college
    admissions, 51; colonial
    meaning of "white," 38;
    discussion, 54–55; education
    system, 32; Jim Crow South,
    47; KKK and power of youth,
    41–44; law's determination
    of who got to be White
    (history), 38–40; overlapping
    institutions, impact of,
    45–46; prejudice, 48–53;
    racial hierarchy, 50; racism,
    definition of, 36; racism
    bigger than KKK, 29–31;
    reverse racism, 50, 51, 52,
    55; scientific racism, 34;
    systemic racism, 31–32, 46;
    top decision makers, 54–55;
    unconscious discrimination,
    49; unequal treatment of races,
    justification of, 33–36; White
    Supremacist, denial of being,
    46–48
systemic racism, 31–32, 46, 187

Takaki, Ronald, 141
talking about race, difficulty of,
    7–28; caste system, definition
    of, 13; children, symbolism
    of colors for, 18; culture,
    lessons of, 18; discussion, 28;
    dominant fragility, 24–27;
    heterosexual mainstream,
    24–26; human ideal, depiction
    of White people as, 15–16;
    identification, 10; media

representations of People of
    Color, 13–14; meritocracy
    and individualism, ideologies
    of, 17–19; privilege, 22–24;
    racial hierarchy, definition
    of, 11–17; segregated
    neighborhoods and schools,
    14–15; socialization, 19–21;
    stereotypical representations,
    14; truncated history, 16–17;
    unique difficulty for White
    people, 7; view of White
    people as raceless, 8–11;
    White children, perception of,
    14; white fragility, definition
    of, 21; White superiority,
    assumptions about, 15
Tatum, Beverly Daniel, 30, 217,
    219
Trump, Donald, 42, 113
Tulsa race massacre, 147
Turner, Brock, 97, 98

unconscious anti-Blackness, 149
unconscious bias, 63, 64, 230
unconscious discrimination, 49
unconscious superiority, 82
Underground Railroad (WBAI),
    110
"undocumented immigrant," 140
*Unraveling the Model Minority
    Stereotype: Listening to Asian
    American Youth*, 143
*Up Against Whiteness: Race,
    School, and Immigrant
    Youth*, 143
US Constitution, right supposedly
    guaranteed in, 24

violent crime, 93
Voting Rights Act of 1965, 24, 60

The Warmth of Other Suns, 12
Washington, George, 16
wealth accumulation, disparities
    in, 62

White archetypes, 205–206; assumed affluent, 205; family tied, 205; the hero, 205; the intellectual, 206; the manipulator, 206; the romantic, 206

white fragility: common condition of, 179; common impacts of, 179; definition of, 21; dominant group and, 26; impacts of, 179; patterns of, 79; predictability of, 225; racial patterns of, 104–106; roots of, 169; rules of engagement, 180; source of, 73; triggers activating, 157; as wall of resistance, 168

white fragility, appearance of and obstruction by, 168–185; assumptions, 176–178; behaviors, 171; blame-placing trajectory, 168; correct question, 181; crying, 184–185; defensive justifications, 174–175; discussion, 185; feedback, necessity of, 183; feelings, 170; "flight" response, 173; impacts of white fragility, 179; marginalized identities, 176; preferred anti-racist response, 182–183; racial bias, assumptions about, 176, 177; roots of white fragility, 169; rules of engagement, 180

white fragility, defining, 152–167; bullying, 154; capacity to handle stress, 155; children's developed sense of White superiority, 161; defensiveness, forms of, 156; defensive rejection displayed by White people, 154, 156; denial of racism, 164; development of white fragility, 161; discussion, 167; ideologies,

challenge to, 156; internalized superiority, 156; moral reputation, protection of, 163; n-word, permission to use, 161; oversensitivity, 153–154; racial comfort of White people, 155; racial stress, White people dealing with, 166; stereotypes, perpetuation of, 166; superiority, White denial of White superiority, 161; triggers, 157

White Nationalists, 41

White people, effect of race on lives of, 79–107; belonging and freedom, 85–88; Christian church, 94; conflict avoidance, 102; crayon color, 83; educated person, 82; gentrification, 96; Ghetto Tracker app, 92, 94; good old days, 88–90; justice system, racial bias and, 98; just people, 81–84; Juveniles of Color, behavior of, 98; minoritized status, 86; mistakes of White youth, forgiveness of, 97; nonviolent crimes, 98; racialized status, 86; redlining, 91; schools, "good" vs. "bad," 93; segregated lives, 90–96; unconscious superiority, 82; violent crime, 93; White children, wealth passed down to, 91; white fragility, racial patterns of, 104–106; Whiteness, normalized, 86; Whiteness, placement on false hierarchy, 83; White racial innocence, 97–100; White solidarity (collusion), 100–103; "windows and mirrors," 82

White-people's kryptonite, 112, 160

White Rage: The Unspoken Truth of Our Racial Divide, 116

Dr. Robin DiAngelo is an affiliate associate professor of education at the University of Washington who also holds two honorary doctorates. She is a two-time winner of the Student's Choice Award for Educator of the Year at the University of Washington's School of Social Work. She is the author of numerous articles and books on racial justice, including *What Does It Mean to Be White?* (2012) and *Nice Racism* (2021). In 2011 she coined the term "white fragility" in an academic article, which has influenced the international dialogue on race. Her book *White Fragility: Why It's So Hard for White People to Talk About Racism* (2018) debuted on the *New York Times* best-seller list, where it remained for over three years. It has been translated into eleven languages. In addition to her academic work, Robin has been a consultant and trainer for over twenty years on issues of racial and social justice. She lives in Seattle.

Toni Graves Williamson, a diversity practitioner and consultant, is director of equity and inclusion at Friends Select School in Philadelphia. She specializes in developing student leadership and programming for grades pre-K through twelve. Toni is a principal consultant of the Glasgow Group, a consortium of school educators that provides professional development and coaching to schools and other organizations. She is codirector and facilitator for the Race Institute for K–12 Educators, a nonprofit organization that provides a space for educators to do the deep personal work of understanding their racial identities. She is a contributing author to *The Guide for White Women Who Teach Black Boys* (Corwin Press, 2017) and *Teaching Beautiful Brilliant Black Girls* (Corwin Press, 2021). Toni holds a bachelor's degree from Duke University in political science and two master of education degrees, one from the University of North Carolina at Greensboro and the other from Columbia University. She currently lives in Philadelphia.

Ali Michael, PhD, is the cofounder and codirector of the Race Institute for K–12 Educators and the author of *Raising Race Questions: Whiteness, Inquiry and Education* (Teachers College Press, 2015), winner of the 2017 Society of Professors of Education Outstanding Book Award. She is coeditor of the best-selling *Guide for White Women Who Teach Black Boys* (Corwin Press, 2018), *Teaching Beautiful Brilliant Black Girls* (Corwin Press, 2021), and *Everyday White People Confront Racial and Social Injustice: 15 Stories* (Stylus Press, 2015). Ali sits on the editorial board of the journal *Whiteness and Education.* Her article "What Do White Children Need to Know About Race?," coauthored with Dr. Eleonora Bartoli and appearing in *Independent Schools Magazine,* won the Association and Media Publishing Gold Award for Best Feature Article in 2014. Ali is the coauthor of *Our Problem, Our Path: Collective Anti-racism for White People* (Corwin

Press, 2022). Ali teaches in the diversity and inclusion program at Princeton University and in the Equity Institutes for Higher Education at the University of Southern California. When she is not writing, speaking, or training, Ali strives to be an anti-racist coparent to two amazing kids.

Originally from Brooklyn, New York, **Kevin Soltau** is an Atlanta-based artist and educator. He is best known for his illustrations depicting hip-hop and dancehall culture. Paying homage to his memories of growing up in New York City and his Jamaican heritage, Kevin designs his digital characters to give you a sense of sharing space with them. Kevin is an elementary art teacher and spends his spare time painting with his two sons.

Lauren Kinnard is a graphic facilitator and educator with a decade of elementary and middle school teaching experience. She facilitates sketchnoting workshops for educators, students, parents, and professionals from various industries, and creates illustrations and infographics for schools and businesses. As a diversity practitioner in K–12 schools, she has served as a facilitator within the diversity, equity, and inclusion space. She lives in Los Angeles.